THROWING
HEAT

THROWING HEAT

THE AUTOBIOGRAPHY OF
NOLAN RYAN

NOLAN RYAN AND
HARVEY FROMMER

Doubleday
NEW YORK
1988

DESIGNED BY PETER R. KRUZAN

Library of Congress Cataloging-in-Publication Data
Ryan, Nolan, 1947–
Throwing heat: the autobiography of Nolan Ryan/Nolan Ryan and
Harvey Frommer.
p. cm.
1. Ryan, Nolan, 1947– . 2. Baseball players—United States—
Biography. I. Frommer, Harvey. II. Title.
GV865.R9A3 1988
796.357′092′4—dc19
[B]   87-33074
                                         CIP

ISBN 0-385-24438-X

BG

To Ruth, my parents, my friends and fans,
for all their support through the years

ACKNOWLEDGMENTS

Various people were of great assistance in sharing their time, memories, and perceptions: Martha Lee Ryan, Red Murff, Jim Watson, Hal Lanier, Ron Luciano, Gene Tenace, Davey Lopes, Alan Ashby, Kenny Hand, Milo Hamilton, Larry Dierker, Phil Garner, Yogi Berra, Rob Matwick, Whitey Herzog, Ozzie Smith, Bing Devine, Bob Broeg, Jack Buck, Kip Ingle, Jack Clark, Tom Bannon, Harvey Greene, Dave Winfield, Jeff Torborg, Herb Score, Mike Schmidt, Glenn Wilson, Tom Seaver, Dick Williams, Ray Keyes, David Perez, Reggie Jackson, Brooks Robinson, Dave Duncan, Bobby Grich, Gerry Davis, Pete Rose, Dale Murphy, Bob Knepper, and Brad Mills.

Agents Elaine Markson and Matt Merola believed in the project right from the start and were supportive all the way through. David Gernert, our editor at Doubleday, provided skillful coaching. Lucy Herring of Doubleday was a constant asset throughout the whole project. Myrna Frommer was of invaluable help in interviewing, reading, organizing, and editing. Ruth Ryan provided valuable insights.

My biggest thank you is extended to Harvey Frommer, a very talented writer. He worked in a pressure situation with much drive and dedication.

And of course, the late Lynn Nolan Ryan Sr.

—NOLAN RYAN

CONTENTS

You think of Walter Johnson and Christy Mathewson and the Cy Young Award. I probably won't live to see it, but one day there will be a Nolan Ryan Award for his accomplishments and for his being a straight arrow. Nolan has always honored his start. We have reason down here in Texas to believe. We have so much space here, we know it belongs to God . . . and we know where He is.

> Red Murff,
> former scout for the
> New York Mets

PROLOGUE

When I was young and starting out, I never thought I would pitch as long as I have. Back in 1966, when I first arrived in the major leagues, power pitchers were starting to get out of the game in their early thirties. I guess I've really defied the odds.

Nobody anticipated my being around and being able to throw so hard this long. If I stay healthy I think I can still be pitching until past my forty-second birthday. In 1987 I became the first pitcher to strike out 2,000 or more batters in each league. I also set the record for the most strikeouts in a season by a pitcher forty years or older.

I get a lot of satisfaction out of the fact that I'm still as hard a thrower as there is in the league—either league. The history of power pitchers is that they start losing their velocity by their early thirties. It pleases me that many scouts compare young kids' arms to my arm, which they consider the number one arm.

We are all driven by different motives. To me, the challenge now is change and age. It's a challenge to pitch with age against me. The longer I pitch, the more I'm performing against younger and younger players. There's no doubt in my mind that I don't throw as well as I did ten or fifteen years ago. Now it takes a lot more effort each year to keep myself in shape, but I enjoy working out and feel a real sense of accomplishment in striving always to maintain and improve myself. I will never make excuses that I can't do things on the field because of my age.

Great pitchers have also come through in my time in baseball, a handful of guys who excelled for a long period of time: Steve Carlton, Tom Seaver, Don Sutton, Bob Gibson, Catfish Hunter, and Jim Palmer. And I saw Don Drysdale and Sandy Koufax at the end of their careers. Gossage and Rollie Fingers were among the relievers who excelled for a long period of time.

I've seen players pass through and out of baseball who I had a lot of respect for, players like Jerry Koosman, Reggie Jackson, Pete Rose, Rod Carew, and Joe Rudi.

I hated to see Tom Seaver retire. That means I'm the last one left playing baseball from the 1969 Mets World Championship team. . . .

I remember one day early in that 1969 season when Jim Bunning pitched against the New York Mets. He was in the twilight of his career then, but his pitching was still impressive. Toward the end of the game the announcement was made that he had struck out his 2,500th batter.

"Imagine, 2,500 strikeouts," I said to Tom, who was sitting next to me in the dugout. "What a career accomplishment."

PROLOGUE

"That's for sure, Nolan," Tom said. "He's been a real quality pitcher."

"I wonder what the record is for all time strikeouts."

"Three thousand five hundred and eight," Tom said. He knew all about baseball history and statistics. "And it's held by Walter Johnson."

"Walter Johnson." That was the first time I'd ever heard that name.

"He was one of the greatest pitchers ever, Nolan. He's in the Baseball Hall of Fame."

"Well, I guess he deserves to be there as much as anyone," I told Tom. "Nobody'll ever break that strikeout record. Here's Jim Bunning pitching after all these years and all he's got is 2,500. That Johnson record will probably stand forever."

THROWING HEAT

PART I

·   ·   ·

ALVIN, TEXAS

was born in Refugio, Texas, on January 31, 1947, the youngest of six children. There were Lynda, Mary Lou, Robert, Judy, Jean, and me. When I was only six weeks old, though, the family moved east to Alvin. The company my father worked for, the old Stanlon Oil Company, now Pan American Petroleum, transferred his job to that area. My mother picked Alvin as a place to settle in because of its reputation for good schools and because she loved the town's beautiful spreading live oak trees that are evergreen.

So that's where we settled, where I grew up, and where I still live today.

I never found a place where I wanted to live more than Alvin. I guess if I were a member of the Chamber of Commerce, I'd have trouble selling the place. The weather's lousy. There are big mosquitoes and a lot of humidity in summer, and in winter there are drastic changes in the climate. In 1979 we had 43 inches of rain in two days and 102 inches for the year. I know Alvin is no great attraction to some, but for me it's where my roots are, where I've always been. It's home.

The town was named for Alvin Morgan, a Santa Fe railroad man who built its first house in 1879. Twenty-six miles south of Houston and twenty-nine miles west of Galveston, Alvin had a population of about five thousand when I was a kid. It was a little town with lots of open space. There was a small downtown area with one movie theater. It was, some people say, kind of like the town in the film *The Last Picture Show.* Things closed down in Alvin about 10 P.M., and most of the folks went to bed early and were up and about before the sun rose. There were very few working mothers; fathers worked in the oil fields or as rice farmers or in the cattle business.

My dad, Lynn Nolan Ryan, was a supervisor at the Hastings plant, where they took crude oil and natural gas and produced diesel fuel and other products.

His family had come from Ireland and lived in Texas for over a hundred years, but my mother's family came from Louisiana. My mother, Martha Lee Hancock, is, according to the family, a descendant of John Hancock. So my roots in this country go back pretty far. In my heart I'm a Texan all the way. That's nothing special, though—you won't find many Texans who aren't proud of their Texas heritage.

Until the time I was in the second grade, we lived in big frame houses that we rented. Then we bought the small four-bedroom house on Dezso Drive that my mother still lives in. There were only eight houses on the street back then. The road wasn't paved and there were open fields all around. By that time two of my sisters had gone off to college, so for most of the year there was enough room for the rest of us in the new house.

My father was a big man, about six foot five and 240 pounds. But he was a gentle man, kindly, and extremely devoted to his family. When my two older sisters were nearing time to go to college, he took over the distributorship for the morning paper the Houston *Post* as a second job. All of Alvin was on that route—about fifteen hundred papers. For a good number of years Dad, my brother, Robert, and I would get up at one in the morning and go down to the old abandoned Sinclair service station on the corner of Sealy and Gordon in what is now the old part of Alvin. I'd roll newspapers there at two and three in the morning and be back in bed by four or five. I got quite an education. Oh, there'd be an occasional drunk staggering by from out of the pool hall down the street even though Alvin is in a dry county, selling only beer. And I'd see skunks crawl out of the drainage system to eat the popcorn that people dropped coming out of the movie. I rolled those papers from the time I was in the second grade until I was fourteen and old enough to drive a car and have my own route.

It wasn't until I graduated from high school that we finally gave up the distributorship. My dad had been through some very tough years—delivering the papers, going to his job with Pan American, making his newspaper collections at four-thirty in the afternoon, having to be in bed by eight or nine just to survive that routine. Maybe that's why he was such a heavy smoker, two to three packs of cigarettes a day. In 1968 he had one lung removed. And for the six months before he died in 1970 of lung cancer, it was terrible. Having seen the suffering he experienced, I'm thankful I never had the desire to smoke.

Some people claimed that I developed my arm throwing the Houston *Post*. That was not the case—it was a short throw from a car, and I made the throw backhanded with my left hand while I steered my '52 Chevy with my right. But I did develop the knack of being able to roll and tie fifty newspapers in just about five minutes, and that probably helped me develop strong fingers and wrists.

When I think of my growing-up years, I remember the summers without air conditioning, the heat and humidity, the mosquitoes . . . but it was all part of living in Alvin. We didn't know any different. I was the type of kid who enjoyed whatever was at hand, especially the big sky and the open spaces where we made baseball diamonds and played ball for hours and hours until it got dark.

And, growing up, I always loved animals. I had a brown and white fox terrier named Suzy, and from the time I was a little kid until I graduated from high school, wherever I went—to games, running around in the field, hunting— that dog went with me.

I remember one day Suzy chased a skunk into a pile of brush. She followed the skunk into the brush and I went in after the dog. We both came out of there smelling like a skunk. When we came home, my mom washed the dog and me with big cans of tomato juice. That was a real Texas cure —the only way she could get that skunk smell off of us.

When I was about twelve, I bought my first calf for two

dollars and fifty cents and brought it home in a feed bag. The calf was about two days old. I bottle-fed that calf and raised it till it was about six months old, and then I sold it and bought a couple more calves. From that time on until I went to high school, I always raised calves outside of town in little pastures that I rented.

We grew up with guns—I had a BB gun from the time I was eight years old. My dad would take my brother and me goose- and duck-hunting on occasion. Later, when I got to high school, I'd go hunting in the fall of the year whenever I had the chance. Being out in nature was the thing that always made hunting a source of relaxation for me.

We got our first TV set, a Philco, in 1953, and I remember watching the "Game of the Week" with Dizzy Dean doing the play-by-play. He was colorful. I thought he was great. That was the only baseball we got except what you heard on the radio. Major league baseball was far removed. The only team you could pick up was the St. Louis Cardinals on the 50,000-watt KMOX. The Cardinals had a big following in our area because their Triple A team, the Houston Buffs, would feed players to them, and we could hear about some of the players that had been with Houston. My dad worked so much that he wasn't a big listener to ball games, so neither was I. But when major league baseball came to Houston later on, I really got into the habit of following Colt .45 games, and I would lie in bed on those hot summer nights listening to the radio and picturing the action.

My favorite players at that time, though, were not on Houston, and they were not pitchers. They were outfielders. Hank Aaron was one of them. I admired him because of his power and his durability. I also especially liked Roberto Clemente. He was what I thought an athlete should be—he was driven, and he put every bit of himself into what he was doing. Clemente played the game flat out all the time and seemed always to be in great shape.

My brother, Robert, was something of a hero to me, being a few years older and more advanced in athletics. I'd hang around with Robert and his friends, shag flies for them, sometimes get into a game when they were shy a player. I'd practice a lot with Robert in our backyard. We would pitch to each other. He'd catch me, and I'd catch him.

My first organized sports experience was in Little League. The first field in Alvin was cleared and built by my dad and the other fathers of the kids in the program. I played Little League from the time I was nine years old until I was thirteen. Some of my fondest memories of baseball come from those years.

I had heard that my dad was a pretty fair ballplayer in his time during the Depression. Although he never was involved in any organized sports, he had a lot of natural athletic ability. As a Little League parent, he was always there when I needed him, but he was not like some of the others you hear about, the kind who meddle in games and care more about their kids winning than how they play the game. My dad was just interested in my having a good organized sports experience. Whenever I played ball, Dad would always stay in the background and just take everything in.

Making the Little League team was a thrill for all of us kids in Alvin. When we'd get our caps and uniforms, we'd be so proud, we'd wear the caps to school. That was a big deal. We played our games in the Texas heat in those old heavy flannel uniforms, but no one seemed to pay the weather any heed.

I was a good player, not a great player, although I did pitch a no-hitter in Little League and was on the All-Star team as an eleven- and twelve-year-old. I didn't develop great pitching velocity until my sophomore year in high school. What I could always do, though, was throw a ball farther than the other kids—not harder, just farther. When I was a high school sophomore, I won a contest in a physical education class by throwing a heavy softball 309 feet. But my arm twinged a bit, and I realized I could get hurt doing that. I never threw a ball for distance again.

As Little Leaguers, we always fantasized about playing in the Little League World Series in Williamsport, Pennsylvania. That made making the All-Stars even more exciting. And although our team never went far in tournament play, we always had high expectations.

One year, after our team had been eliminated, I remember standing out on the field for the closing ceremony. The man who was presenting the awards gave a little talk to all of us. "One day," he said, "one of you Little Leaguers will go on to play in the major leagues."

When I heard what he said, it was like a bell went off in my head. I became very excited.

When I got home I told my mom about the ceremony and what the man said. "Mom," I said, "that man was talking about me."

"What do you mean?" she asked.

"It's me that he meant, Mom! I'm sure it was me he was talking about."

I remember that experience as vividly as if it just happened yesterday—the sun, the standing in the field, the man's voice, his words. I never forgot it. It was a monumental thing in my mind.

During that period of my life, whenever I had the chance I would be throwing something, and my mother was always on me for breaking windows or hitting the car. I especially liked going down to Mustang Bayou near our house to throw rocks at the water moccasins and turtles.

Growing up in Alvin allowed me to have a childhood that was uncomplicated and without pressures. And although there were financial pressures on my dad, we always had the things we needed. We grew up not having a lot of extra things but not in want of any either. It was pretty much that way for most all the kids. But my father paid me for the newspaper route, and I mowed yards in the summer, so that I always had money for what I wanted.

Since my dad worked so much, the burden fell on Mom to manage the household. For a time, with eight of us there sleeping two in a room, that was quite a chore. But she was always organized, and the house ran smoothly. Mom was a reserved person, but she was always open with all the kids, ready to talk over any of our problems.

It was a pleasant atmosphere to grow up in. We were all raised to respect other people, to do the right thing, to stand up for our rights, to value the family.

My parents' work ethic and dedication shaped my work ethic and dedication, both to my family and to my pitching. My goal has always been to raise my kids in the same kind of atmosphere that I grew up in—a family doing things for each other and loving each other.

At that time we also belonged to the First Methodist Church in Alvin. It was there that the wisdom of the Bible and the teachings of the church first influenced my life. Lack of vanity and consideration for others are teachings that I have always taken seriously.

RUTH RYAN:

My roots aren't All-American like Nolan's. In fact my grandparents came here from Sweden and my parents grew up in New York City. When my dad came back from World War II, he and my mom lived in Staten Island for a while, but he didn't have much of a job or see much of a future. His father was a sea captain, and he told Dad that there was a lot of opportunity in the Gulf Coast area of Texas around Galveston. So my dad and my mother and my sister, Lynn, who was just a one-year-old baby then, set out by car for Texas. They'd got as far as Alvin when my dad realized all they had left was thirty dollars.

Rather than go on, my dad went into a local appliance store and asked the owner for a job. That man hired him and gave him a house to rent, and that is how they came to Alvin. They never left. I was born the next year, and then came three boys.

My dad still remembers the first time he saw Nolan. He was working on the Ryans' refrigerator and Nolan toddled in; he was about a year old. He took some tools out of my dad's toolbox and went and hid under the bed with them.

My sister, Lynn, was in the same class as Nolan. She thought he was cute, and she would take me with her to the ballpark to watch him play Little League baseball. He was either the pitcher or the shortstop, but nobody noticed that he was different than anybody else.

As far as noticing him as a boyfriend, I guess it was when I was about thirteen. That's when we had our first date, a double date. Since he delivered newspapers, he had his own car, which was rather unusual. There wasn't much for us kids to do except see a movie or go get a Coke. We became boyfriend and girlfriend then and stayed that way throughout high school. There was never anybody else for either of us.

Athletics was one thing that Ruth and I immediately had in common. As a sophomore in high school, Ruth and her friend Rachel Adams won the state tennis doubles championship in their AAA division. They got a lot of attention in Alvin because of that. I tell people that Ruth is the athlete in our family.

Ruth was "All School Most Beautiful" three years running. We spent a lot of nice times together. We'd play basketball and baseball. We'd go driving around town, go to the movies, hang out at Dairyland, the local gathering place for high school kids in Alvin.

I was never the type to confide in too many people, but with Ruth it was different right from the start. She has always been a good listener, she's always been a sensitive person. We became not only boyfriend and girlfriend but close friends. And that's the way it's been through all these years.

One Sunday between my junior and senior years in high school we went to see the Houston Colt .45's play the Los Angeles Dodgers. Sandy Koufax was pitching, and I was a big Koufax fan. It was the first time I had a box seat without slipping into one with a general admission ticket. It was the first time I had ever seen Sandy pitch. I was truly amazed at how fast he was and how good a curveball he had. I think he was the most overpowering pitcher I have ever seen.

Those high school days were very pleasant times. I experienced special moments and some of the happiest days of my life then. There were under six hundred kids in the whole high school, and you knew almost everyone. My attitude at that time was that I went to school to play sports. Now I wish I had paid more attention to my studies.

All I thought about in high school was basketball. I was six foot two, but I was the center on the team because I was a good jumper. We were 27–4 two years in a row. I felt like I could have played small-college basketball, and that's what

I wanted to do. I remember that one of the colleges, I think it was San Jacinto, held basketball tryouts in our area just as the baseball season was beginning. I was scheduled to pitch on the day of the tryout. I wanted to go and would have if I hadn't been pitching.

A friend and teammate of mine, Darrel Hunt, did wind up going. In fact, he later played college ball, but they ruled him ineligible for high school baseball that season because of it. I often think about that. If I'd gone to that tryout, I don't know what would've happened. It's funny the turns your life will take. . . .

JIM WATSON:

I was Nolan's high school baseball coach. He never did weigh more than 150 pounds then, but even as a skinny kid he could throw that ball through a wall. He was quiet, a good student, probably the most unpretentious young man I've ever seen. Nolan was very raw as a high school pitcher, didn't have a curveball. His first two years on the team, he couldn't go four or five innings on the mound. We didn't know how fast he was —we had no guns.

Still, he had a fireball. I swear that ball jumped eight inches when it reached the plate. And he was wild. There were problems with catchers who were afraid to catch him or couldn't hold on to his ball, it moved so much—there were quite a few passed balls. Nolan didn't have any idea where the ball was going, but he didn't exactly have to thread the needle back then. Those kids were so scared, they'd swing at anything just to get out of there. Once he broke a player's wrist, and once a kid just refused to come up and hit against him. He'd average fifteen, sixteen strikeouts sometimes in those seven-inning games.

In Texas, back in the sixties, football was king. We only played baseball because the state made us. The major leagues to us in Alvin were a million miles away.

To tell the truth, I didn't know what I had. I had played football for the University of Texas, and no one ever accused me of having a lot of knowledge of baseball techniques. But I could motivate. My only claim to fame with Nolan is that I kept him in shape, didn't hurt his arm, and made sure he was ready to go. I also taught him a mental toughness that has never left him.

RED MURFF:

In 1963 I began working for the New York Mets as a scout after a time with the Houston Colt .45s. One Saturday morning, the first weekend in March, I was scouting in Galveston.

As it happened, I had about an hour to pass on my way from Galveston to another scouting assignment that afternoon in Houston. So I figured I'd watch a high school baseball tournament in Alvin just to see who was winning.

There was just one other scout there—Mickey Sullivan, who worked for the Philadelphia Phillies. It was the second or third inning of the game and I didn't even know who was playing. Mickey told me it was Alvin High playing somebody, Clear Lake or Clear Creek. The Alvin coach was changing pitchers just about the time I got settled in.

This skinny, handsome right-hander threw two fastball

strikes—and I was thunderstruck. You could hear that ball explode. Then he threw an atrocious curveball and the hitter doubled to right center.

"Who's that kid out there?" I asked Mickey Sullivan.

"Nolan Ryan," he answered. "He doesn't have too much, does he?"

"I don't know . . ." I said. Then I started to bite my tongue. "He doesn't have a very good curveball," I added. That's the closest I've ever come to being a liar.

That night I went to the old Colt Stadium and saw Turk Farrell of Houston and Jim Maloney of the Cincinnati Reds pitch against each other in the twilight. They could both throw ninety-five-mile-per-hour fastballs. At high noon that young man I had seen threw harder than either of them. I'm a hunter and I know something about ballistics, and when I filled out my report for the New York Mets I said that Ryan was in the hundred-mile-per-hour range, that his ball stayed level in flight, rose as it got to the plate, and then exploded.

At the end of Nolan's sophomore year I took it upon myself to inform Alvin's athletic director and Jim Watson what they had. I knew the way it was in Texas high schools, how they grabbed a sophomore with a lean, lithe body and put him on a weight-training program, so that before he became a senior he was muscle-bound. Knowing this, I made my first threat ever to an athletic director and a coach.

"You-all have one of the ten best arms in the world, in your school," I told them.

"You mean ———?" Jim asked.

"No," I answered.

"Oh, then you mean —————."

"I mean Nolan Ryan."

"Nolie? I can't believe this, Mr. Murff." Jim didn't even dream I was talking about Ryan because Nolan had some troubles pitching in high school.

"If you put Nolan Ryan on a weight program to make him stronger and I hear about it, I'm gonna get all the scouts to sit in your park and we're gonna get your job," I told the athletic director. "You'll make a big mistake if you try and tamper with that arm."

The athletic director didn't put up any fight. "Red," he said, "you sure as shootin' know more about pitching a baseball than I do. I'll go along with whatever you say."

"Don't bulk him up," I told the athletic director. "Just let him throw a baseball. You do what I say, and it'll be good for you, good for me, and especially good for Nolan."

Then I turned to Jim Watson. "Have Nolan throw only fastballs with runners on second and third. Always have confidence in him, and you'll play your last ball game of the season in Austin, Texas."

"Austin's not in our conference," Jim said.

Jim Watson didn't look far enough ahead then. Austin is where the top Texas high school baseball teams wind up in the state finals.

I had a close friend, Robert "Red" Gaskell, and he was my bird dog, my sub-scout, back then. "Your assignment," I told him, "is to watch Nolan Ryan pitch. Wherever he goes, you go!"

JIM WATSON:

I remember after that game when Red Murff saw Nolan for the first time, he came over to me all charged up. "That skinny kid —what is he—a senior?"

"Nope," I told him. "He's tall for his age, but he's only a sophomore."

"You know, Jim, I never seen an arm like that in my life."

"I haven't either," I said. "That Nolie's throwing the ball all over the place." That was how smart I was.

"Can I talk to him?" Red asked.

"I don't see where it'll do any harm, Red."

That was the beginning. From that time on, Red and his bird dog just haunted Nolan. Red also asked me to do him a favor —although he denies it now.

"Don't send any of your scores in to the Houston papers, Jim," he said, "and don't give Nolan any undue publicity."

"What's the point of that?" I asked.

"I think too much attention will only break his concentration," Red said.

I went along with granting Red Murff his favor. So Nolan did not really get that much publicity. Only by word of mouth did he become a myth—"that kid from Alvin who could throw the ball so hard you could hardly see it."

I was so tall and skinny and raw during high school. That's why I didn't pay much heed to being scouted—I had no idea that I could ever play in the big leagues. I remember going to the Astrodome the year it opened in 1965, my senior year in high school. I watched those major leaguers play. They were so much older and more polished than I was. I never considered myself on their level.

Baseball was something we did in the spring and summer. It was fun. Our team's season rode on my shoulders. We would go as far as I took them—we had very little hitting.

Throughout high school I was in my own world, having fun on Friday and Saturday nights, playing ball. Going to the majors wasn't a big item as far as I was concerned. But there might have been more excitement in the community of Alvin than I was aware of, what with Red Murff and Red Gaskell being around a lot of the time watching me pitch. Still, there was no pressure. Red Gaskell, to me, was just a guy who lived over in Texas City, who had a full-time job and on his off-time was around me a lot. I looked at Red Gaskell and what he was doing as simply a guy supplementing his income.

Other scouts came through and checked me out and didn't have the interest. There were no radar guns—I didn't know how fast I was. I was so wild. I was just a kid with a great arm. I didn't know what I had. No one did—only Red Murff.

RED MURFF:

During that time Nolan developed blisters, and I recommended that he use Tuff Skin, a lacquer-type substance for blisters and stuff. The Tuff Skin affected his control even more. Some of the scouts said, "That Red Murff is giving stuff to

Ryan to keep him from throwing hard." But they all missed him. They all walked by Nolan and told his dad to send him to college.

JIM WATSON:

I knew how to put a team together, but I didn't know anything about teaching pitching. And I was real macho then, or at least I thought I was. I wouldn't even let the players rub the sore spots where balls hit them. . . .

One time during Nolan's senior year, our team suffered two straight 1–0 losses, and I got real mad at our boys, so I had them all out running the next day. I also had Nolan pitch thirty minutes of batting practice. I don't know what bothered them more—the running, or Nolan's fastball.

Later that same day Red Murff came to me all excited. He told me that Bing Devine, then head of scouting for the New York Mets, was coming to town to take a look at Nolan pitching.

"Red," I said, "Nolan can't go. I ran him today until he puked green. Can't we do it another day?"

"This is the only time Devine will be down here," Red said. "You gotta pitch him."

BING DEVINE:

Red Murff was a dedicated and capable scout, and he was fiercely jealous about his scouting recommendations. That was good—you like that about a scout. He kept sending in written reports and we had several phone conversations about

Nolan Ryan. So I came down to Texas to see Ryan with high expectations.

Red picked me up at the airport and we drove to Channelview, where Alvin was playing. "You're gonna like him," Red told me. "This Ryan kid is the greatest pitching prospect I've ever seen. Wait till you see him pitch!" He kept building Nolan up.

We arrived at Channelview and went to the baseball field in back of the school. It had a small diamond and simple stands. There was nothing sophisticated at all about the environment. It was like a thousand other small-town baseball fields I had been to. The day was warm, but I had spent a lot of time in St. Louis, so I was used to that kind of weather.

Well, Ryan pitched, and he was bad. He just had a miserable day. We didn't have radar guns in those days, so we relied on the scout's eye and his personal analysis of how hard a pitcher threw. The way I checked to see if a pitcher threw hard was to see if the opposing hitters made contact at all, if they even hit foul balls. If the hitters at that level of play made contact, then you realized that the pitcher wasn't as fast as he appeared. Not only was Ryan wild that day, but the other team hit the ball. The team made considerable contact.

I noticed when Red Murff and Bing Devine came into the stands at the beginning of the game. I was nervous and real anxious to do well. I pitched even though I had nothing. I only pitched to the third inning, and I was trailing 7–0. It was the worst kind of showing I could have had, and I thought for sure I had blown my chance.

BING DEVINE:

We left when Nolan was taken out of the game. When we got into the car, Red Murff was almost in tears. "The kid had a bad day," he said. "You just didn't see what he's got in him. He wasn't even supposed to pitch. I convinced the coach to have him pitch so you could see him."

"Well, I saw him all right," I said.

"What do we do now?" Murff asked. "You gonna knock me out of the box?"

And this is where I take a little of the credit. "I know I'm not as good a scout as you are, Red," I told him. "And I also know that by seeing a player one time you can be fooled good or bad. You've been seeing this fellow for three years in high school. You know what he can do. Obviously I won't be able to corroborate your great report when we sit at a meeting up there in New York City and set up our list of draft choices. But I won't fight it. I'll just say that Red Murff says Ryan is better than I saw him, and he undoubtedly is."

RED MURFF:

Driving back to Houston with Bing Devine in my car took a long time. The circumstances made it seem even longer. The traffic was pretty bad, and I was afraid my scouting judgment looked the same. Devine had been a top man in baseball for many years, and I had a lot of respect for him. But I also knew that Nolan had the goods, and I trusted my own judgment.

"Red," he said to me, "I'll tell you what I'm going to do. I'm going to send you around the country to see five really good arms so that you'll get some more perspective on this boy."

I circled around for a few weeks, and I looked at pitchers that Devine had recommended. Then I reported back. "Mr. Devine," I said, "those arms are all pretty good. But I'm damn certain none of them count a lick compared to Nolan Ryan's."

BING DEVINE:

I give Red full credit for what he did. He was so insistent. He just wouldn't let us negate the whole thing. You can't overdramatize what happened. It has the ring of fiction. Scouting, you know, is not an exact science. Sometimes you have to go by instinct, by a feeling. Fortunately, I went along with Murff. I guess I didn't go with him extremely strong and we didn't draft Ryan as high as he deserved, but we did draft Nolan Ryan, and it was all because of Red.

RED MURFF:

The New York Mets wound up drafting Ryan in the eighth round in 1965. He was the 295th player taken in the draft. The thought that the best arm that I'd ever seen was taken so low deeply bothered me. But I knew what we had. And I was intent on signing him.

I was pretty disappointed being picked as the 295th player. It was like they were sending me a message that they thought 294 high school players had a better chance of making the majors than I did. All along, Red Murff had been building me up, telling me how great I was, but I had no one to really compare myself to. I actually didn't even understand what the major league draft was and how it worked, and I was not convinced that I had the ability or the desire to play major league baseball.

RED MURFF:

Steve Vernon, a former farmer who had gone to college and became a sportswriter in Texas City, got the Ryans' okay to sit in on our signing discussions. The Ryans set down two conditions: first, that Steve would not be allowed to reveal the amount of the signing without their permission, and second, that Steve was welcome to their home to watch and listen, but he could have no input in the discussion.

I met with Nolan and his family once. Then we met again. Nolan was uncertain about what he wanted to do with his life. He didn't know whether he should get a full-time job, go on to college, or sign with the New York Mets. He was a tough sell. Our third meeting took place June 28, 1965. I recall it was a lovely Texas evening. We sat around the kitchen table: Nolan, his mother, his father, the sportswriter Vernon, and me.

"Major leaguers make so much money, I'm almost embarrassed to talk about it," I told Nolan. "You can make $150,000 a year if you're real good." Little did either of us imagine he would one day make a million dollars a year.

The Met offer was a good bundle of cash for an eighth-round pick. With incentives and a college scholarship, the total package reached about $30,000. We talked some and then I gave him the pen.

"It's your turn, Nolan," I said. "It's your turn to get on the mound now." He sat there and reached for the pen, then shied away from it like it had some electric current in it. Then he rubbed his hands and stared at that old pen. We sat there in that house with all the memories of Nolan's growing-up years, his plaques and trophies from Little League and high school sports, but Nolan did not pick that pen up. I'd been through it all before with signings. You just wait.

All the attention that Red and his sub-scout had given me and all the things they told me about my potential made me look forward to the draft. I knew I had made a poor showing when Bing Devine came down to see me. Still, in truth, my pride was hurt at my not being picked higher than I was. That was one of the reasons I hesitated.

But then I looked across the table at my father. I could tell he wanted me to sign. I thought of how I was the last of the six children he had raised and worked so hard for. I thought of all the hard years of delivering newspapers while most people slept. I thought of the price he had paid doing things for his family.

RED MURFF:

"Your mom and dad are waiting for you to sign, Nolan," I said. "It's on the table." The atmosphere in that house was like a ballpark in the bottom of the ninth inning with the bases loaded, two outs, and a 3–2 count on the batter. Everybody sitting there knew that something had to give.

What gave was Steve Vernon. He forgot his neutral-observer vow. "What's the matter with you, boy?" he cried, jumping out of his chair and throwing his hands in the air. "You crazy? Sign!"

I didn't bring Vernon around for that purpose, but he sure as shootin' put the finishing touches on the deal. Nolan signed.

PART II

NEW YORK

was eighteen years old and had never been away from home when I signed up to play for the New York Mets. They assigned me to Marion, Virginia, in the Appalachian League, a rookie league. Their season started late so that high school and college players signed after graduation would have a place to play. My mother and Ruth went with me to the airport in Houston, and I took my first plane ride.

I felt lonely, a little scared, and terribly uncertain about what was going to happen to me. All my loved ones were left behind, and here I was out on my own for the first time in my life.

My manager at Marion was Pete Pavelick. He was a kind man who tried to ease some of the problems of the kids assigned to the team. We had forty or more players on our roster. All of them had been stars back home. At Marion they had to struggle to survive and not be cut. We only suited up twenty players for games, while the others stayed behind to practice against each other. If you didn't play well, there was always another guy waiting to take your place. There were a lot of busted dreams and guys who cried when they were sent home. It was cruel, survival of the fittest, but I learned early that was the way of life in professional sports.

I rented a bedroom from a widow woman who worked at the bank in Marion. She rented out three bedrooms in the upstairs of her house. I never was so homesick in my life.

Marion had never had a professional baseball team before that season, and the town was in the process of building a park. In the meantime we played in a makeshift place but drew pretty well—almost a thousand a game in a town that had a population of about six thousand.

Dim lights, a rough field, small and cramped dressing rooms, showers with no hot water, long bus rides—all of that was new to me, but that was the atmosphere at Marion and all minor league ball.

Those days at Marion gave me my first experiences with road trips and having to handle a lot of time on my hands. I was fortunate that my background and upbringing had given me a solid foundation.

I had a roommate, Roger Hennington, from Sunnyvale, California. He was only seventeen years old, also a pitcher, and just about as green as I was. One night we were in Harlan, Kentucky, staying in a room on the bottom floor of the hotel. Our room faced the alley and the hotel wasn't air-conditioned, so we kept the windows wide open.

About midnight Roger and I heard a knock on the screen. Two hookers were out there. They explained that the house security was in the lobby of the hotel and wouldn't let them come in. They asked if we'd do them a favor and let them come into the hotel through our room.

Roger and I helped those gals crawl in through the window, which they used as an entrance to the hotel. Then about two o'clock in the morning the hookers knocked on our door. They went through our room and exited from the hotel by crawling back out through the window. I thought how life had changed from the way it was in Alvin.

Our team didn't have enough uniforms to go around, and I was with Marion a few days before I was even issued one. It had belonged to a player who was released. He was a real big guy and I had to get it altered to fit me.

That summer of 1965 more than seventy players passed through the Marion roster. I lasted the whole season. Pitching in 13 games, I won 3 and lost 6. I also struck out 115 batters in 78 innings. In the dim light, to a lot of nervous kids, I guess I was a little dangerous to hit against. I gave up 56 walks and hit 8 batters.

Even though I was erratic, Pavelick was impressed with me and sent in positive reports to the Mets. They invited me to play in St. Petersburg, Florida, over the winter in the instructional league. Only the top twenty prospects in the Mets' organization were given that opportunity, and I felt like I was making some progress.

At St. Pete it was a low-pressure deal. I'd only pitch about five innings a game, and they didn't bother keeping records or anything like that. Mornings were set aside for practice—and in the afternoons we played games.

Eddie Stanky managed St. Pete in the instructional league that year. He was also the head of the minor league department for the Mets. Stanky was very stern and almost

military-like in his approach to fundamentals and conditioning. Coming into contact with him gave me my first
introduction to the mental side of the game. It was also my
first experience with a pitching coach. I realized that I had
a long ways to go to be a big league pitcher.

The spring of 1966 I went to minor league spring training at Homestead, Florida. I remember that time as the
first time I saw Tom Seaver. He had been in a special pool
drawing and the Mets had drawn his name out of a hat and
he became their property. When Tom came to spring training in Homestead, he was assigned to the Jacksonville AAA
team, and I was assigned to Greenville, a class A team. I
think this shows pretty clearly where the two of us were at
that time in our development as pitchers.

I broke camp with the Greenville team and headed to
South Carolina in the Class A Western Carolina League for
the 1966 season. I knew the level of play would be better
than it had been in the Appalachian League, but I knew I
would be better, too. I had learned a little bit more about
how to pitch in the instructional league. And going into
that spring, I was starting to fill out. My weight had shot up
to 170 pounds.

I earned six hundred dollars a month at Greenville, a
hundred dollars more than the year before, but the conditions in my second season were worse than in the Appalachian League. Greenville was a sleepy town of about sixty
thousand people, and we drew only about seven hundred
or so fans to a game. There wasn't much to do in Green-

ville, and I was bored most of the time. I missed Ruth and my family a lot.

The dressing rooms in Greenville were under the stands. They were dirty and cramped and you had to wait your turn to dress and undress—that's how small and cluttered it was. I had gotten used to the conditions—two showers and no hot water. It was the same as in Marion. Some of our trips on those old, broken-down buses lasted almost eight hours, and the conditions in some of those ballparks on the road were even worse than those at Greenville: awful rough fields, poor lighting, no showers. We played every other day at home, so our road trips were one day, every other day. This put us on the bus a lot more than we should have been.

My wildness was still with me. In one game a pitch got away from me and hit a woman who was leaning up against the screen behind home plate. Unfortunately, that wild pitch broke her arm. The woman was a season ticket holder with a good seat up close to the action. Realizing she had a wild-armed kid like me to contend with, she didn't want to take any chances, so she switched her seat to one farther from home plate.

That summer my parents, my youngest sister, and Ruth came down to see me. I was real excited about pitching for them again and maybe I put a little extra on the ball. Pitching against Gastonia, I struck out nineteen. That was a seven-inning game, so all but two of the outs I recorded came on strikeouts.

It was about that time that some of the newspapers began comparing me to Sandy Koufax. It was flattering, and I was pleased, but inside of me I knew that the hitters in the Western Carolina League were just overmatched against my fastball. I also knew that I was in no way a complete pitcher, even though I had a great year with Greenville. I struck out 272 in 183 innings. I won 17 games—the most in the league—and lost only 2 games—the least in the league. I also had control problems, giving up 127 walks, the most of any other pitcher in the league. The hitters helped me out by swinging at a lot of bad pitches. As far as learning to pitch, I made very little progress.

All in all, I consider my year at Greenville as one of the most pleasant I've ever had in baseball. It was, over all, a very successful season for me. Pete Pavelick was my manager again, and that was a plus.

And I leased a house across from a city park with three other players and we had some good times there. With all the parties and the people that were constantly coming and going, that place was more like a fraternity house than anything else. I could feel myself maturing as a young adult. I also felt something building that year, as I was on my way toward becoming a legitimate major league prospect.

After the Western Carolina season ended, I was promoted to Williamsport, Pennsylvania, in the AA Eastern League. I never got to the Little League World Series there, but at least I did play in Williamsport for ten days. A lot of unusual things happened in those ten days. I struck out quite a few batters—thirty-five in nineteen innings.

Unfortunately, I sent my catcher, Duffy Dyer, off the field on a stretcher with a concussion after I hit him in the head with a change-up when he was warming me up. And on September 1, 1966, I had the greatest game of my career up to that point in time. Against Pawtucket, I struck out nineteen batters in nine innings. Dave Nelson stole home and gave Pawtucket an unearned run in the sixth. And in the tenth inning Don Gadbury bunted his way on and moved to second when I threw the ball away. Then Gadbury moved up to third on a passed ball by Duffy Dyer, who was always a little gun-shy of my pitches. I had a 3–2 count on the batter when Gadbury stole home. I wound up with twenty-one strikeouts but lost the game 2–1.

I was very excited about what I had accomplished in the minors, but I was even more excited by the thought of pitching in the majors, throwing against major league hitters. I'd been told that I would join the Mets after September 1—the date major league teams called up prospects from the minors for the final month of the season—and I was looking forward to trying out my fastball against top hitters.

In my last start with Williamsport I was scheduled to pitch just four innings and then get on a plane and fly to LaGuardia Airport to join the New York Mets.

I had a no-hitter going for four innings.

When I returned to the dugout, my Williamsport manager, Bill Virdon, told me, "You've got to be going to report to the Mets, but you've given up no hits. Do you want to continue pitching in this game and go for the no-hitter?"

"Mr. Virdon," I told him, "if it's all right with you, I'd just as soon move on along to New York City." The no-hitter, to my mind, was secondary to my joining the New York Mets.

"Okay, Nolan," Virdon said. "Go on your way. Good luck to you."

It had been a whirlwind fourteen months for a nineteen-year-old from Alvin, Texas: Marion, Virginia, in the Appalachian Rookie League; Greenville, South Carolina, in the Western Carolina League; Williamsport, Pennsylvania, in the Eastern League. And now the New York Mets and the National League.

The 1966 Mets were a bad ball club. The team was managed by the former New York Giant catcher Wes Westrum. Its pitchers included Dick Selma, Bob Friend, and Jack Fisher. The infield had Ed Kranepool at first base, Ron Hunt at second, Eddie Bressoud at short, and the former Cardinal Ken Boyer at third. Not one player on the Mets hit .300 that year, and not one of their pitchers had a won-lost record much above .500. The team finished next to last in the National League standings—almost thirty games behind the pennant-winning Los Angeles Dodgers.

My first season in the majors was the final season for Sandy Koufax—and he went out in a blaze, leading all major league pitchers in wins, earned run average, and strikeouts.

I was excited to be in New York City but also a bit awed by the whole thing. I had come all the way from A ball to the major leagues in one season and had attracted a lot of fanfare. Players would say, "Wait till you see this kid Ryan pitch. Wait till you see his arm." And I felt like I had to go out there and show everybody how hard I could throw. It was the mentality of the gunfighter, the fastest gun in the West.

I guess it was kind of easy for Wes Westrum to pick that up. "Nolan, you're up here just for us to take a look at you," he told me. "Your major league future does not depend on how you do. We just want you to relax, and when I call on you to pitch, just do the best you can."

Westrum's words helped me relax a bit, but only just a bit. Shea Stadium was a noisy place, with jets always roaring overhead from LaGuardia Airport. That was unsettling. The Mets drew about 25,000 a game—five times more people than *lived* in Alvin. That was also unsettling. When the games began, I would sit out in the bullpen with the extra catchers and relief pitchers. And sometimes my mind would drift back to thoughts of home, my family, and Ruth.

My first major league appearance was on September 11, 1966, against the Atlanta Braves. I had a big case of stage fright walking out of the bullpen and stepping on the mound, knowing I would be pitching to players like Hank Aaron, Eddie Mathews, and Joe Torre. Being on the mound in the majors was a moment I had dreamed about, but it was also a moment that darn near made me throw up— that's how scared I was.

But I got through it, giving up a home run to Joe Torre

but also getting my first major league strikeout. The batter was Pat Jarvis, a rookie pitcher for Atlanta.

That first time on a major league mound was a big learning experience for me. Hank Aaron said I had one of the best fastballs he had ever seen. But one of the best fastballs I'd ever thrown was hit for a home run by Joe Torre. I learned the hard way that it would not be possible to get by in the major leagues with just a fastball, no matter how hard it was thrown.

It dawned on me that I'd been force-fed to the Mets and that I would have to channel my abilities—be not just a thrower but a pitcher. I really needed guidance, somebody to work with me not only on the physical approach to pitching but also on the mental game. I was just out there stumbling about. If I hadn't had the ability and the determination to work to develop myself, I would've been just another one of those kids that comes along with a great arm. And two years after they sign with a major league team they just fade out into the sunset and people ask, "Whatever happened to that kid?" I was determined that something like that would not happen to me. I spent a lot of time observing, picking up whatever insights I could get into the art of pitching.

The last road trip of the 1966 season was going to take the Mets into Houston. Before we left, Wes Westrum called me into his office. "You know, Nolan," he said, "this team is just playing out the string and looking forward to the future. When we get to Houston, I'm planning on giving you a start. I know we're rushing you, but management wants to see if you can be counted on for next season."

"That's fine with me, sir," I told him. I was very excited, and I rushed to a telephone and called home to give my parents the news.

That first major league start in the Dome is one that I remember very well even though I did not do what I wanted to. My own cheering section was there—Ruth, my parents, my sisters, Jim Watson, and a lot of my following from my high school days.

I was nineteen years old and nervous as all get out. And I was overthrowing. I pitched only one inning. Wes Westrum took me out for a pinch hitter after I'd given up three runs.

It was very disappointing. I don't think any rookie should ever start his first major league game in his own hometown. There was a lot of traffic around the Astrodome that day and some of my friends who came to see me pitch never even got the chance because when they finally managed to get into the ballpark, I was gone.

I wound up my first full season in organized baseball striking out 313 batters in 205 innings in three leagues. And that was fine. But I knew I had a lot to learn about pitching.

That winter I enrolled at Alvin Junior College, even though I thought that I probably wouldn't complete the semester because I was on the waiting list to get into the Army Reserve six-month deal. I did complete the semester, though, and just after New Year's Day of 1967 I left Alvin once again and headed out into the world on my own and put on an Army uniform. My six months were spent at Fort Jackson in Columbia, South Carolina, and Fort Leonard Wood, Missouri. When I finished my active duty, the Mets assigned me to Jacksonville, Florida, their Triple A team in the International League.

First, however, the Mets sent me to Winter Haven, in the Florida State League, to work out. After two weeks there I reported to Jacksonville, where Bill Virdon was the manager. I went on a long road trip with the team as soon as I arrived. Virdon had me pitch in relief, and I did quite well, getting eighteen of twenty-one outs on strikeouts.

In one of those appearances I came into a game and my forearm was very tight. Out of stupidity, I just kept throwing. Then I felt something pop in my arm—just like a rubber band. Bill had to take me out of the game. When I was checked out later, no one was too concerned about the condition of my arm. A little rest, it seemed, was all I would need.

WHITEY HERZOG:

I was the director of player development for the Mets then, and whenever I came into contact with Nolan I thought he was a lazy Texan. He always seemed to be sleeping on the bench when I was talking. I guess he just didn't want to hear my bullshit.

At Jacksonville in 1967 Ryan was set to make his first start for the team. Bing Devine, then the Met general manager, told me, "You better get down there, Whitey, and see that everything goes all right."

> They had people stacked fifty deep in the outfield waiting to
> see him pitch. His strikeout record had preceded him. They
> never had a crowd as big as that down there even for the
> Gator Bowl.

"My arm still bothers me," I told Bill Virdon before the
game was to start. "I don't think I can pitch."

"Go down and warm up, Nolan," he said. "And if you
can't pitch, we'll get someone else."

I went down and tried to warm up. It was no go. I
couldn't throw the ball more than ten feet without my arm
killing me.

WHITEY HERZOG:

> When I saw the way Ryan was throwing the ball, I knew there
> was no way he would be able to pitch that game. Bill Virdon
> knew the score, too. He pulled Ryan and substituted Larry
> Bearnarth as the starter.

The Jacksonville general manager, who was also the
owner of the team, came rushing in ranting and raving.
"There's such a big crowd here," he said, "these people
came out just to see Ryan." He turned to Virdon. "Bill, at
least let him go out to home plate and apologize to all the
people that he can't pitch."

"He's not going to do that," Virdon said. "We'll just get
somebody on the mike and tell the people what happened
and offer to give them their money back."

WHITEY HERZOG:

> The announcement was made and the crowd booed and was pissed off, and there wasn't two hundred people that stayed to watch the game. That was the kind of draw Ryan was already and an indication of the kind of draw he would be one day in the majors.

That 1967 season was a disaster for me. I didn't pitch again that whole season and I didn't know if I would ever be able to throw again. However, on June 26, 1967, in Alvin, Ruth and I were married. That definitely was the highlight of my year.

RUTH RYAN:

> We had a fairly large wedding in the Methodist church in Alvin. I don't remember all that much about it because my mother did most of the planning. I was still in high school. I got married about a month after graduation. Nolan asked for Monday off. We got married Monday night. And he had to go right back to Jacksonville because they had a game the next night. So the day after the wedding we went to Florida. We had this tiny apartment with nothing in it. We went to the dime store and bought two pillows for ninety-nine cents. And then the next day Nolan left on a two-week road trip. I was never so miserable in my life. I didn't know a single person. I called home to wish my dad a happy birthday and started crying. I was ready to go back home. I thought, If this is baseball, I don't like it.
>
> I stayed there for July and August and then came home to

start school. Nolan was home for just a couple of weeks and then he left to play winter ball because he had a hurt arm and had to go down there and try to pitch some and rehabilitate a little bit. He was gone all that year. We were married, but we weren't together.

Then I left Alvin to be with him that summer of 1968. He had been moved up to the majors, and so we lived in New York. At first we stayed at a motel near Shea Stadium, then we had an apartment in a high-rise in Elmhurst, and then one in Bayside, both of which are in the borough of Queens. I couldn't get used to New York. Once I took the car out for a ride. I planned to drive around so I could get to know the city. The rain was pouring down. The windshield wipers didn't work, and I had to keep opening the door to see where the yellow line was. There was so much traffic. That was an end to my exploring.

New York was so different from what we were used to in Alvin. I was only nineteen and I didn't know anyone. I had some family in Staten Island and New Jersey, and my grandmother lived in Brooklyn. They were all nice to me, they invited me over and all, but still I was alone most of the time.

In Alvin, whenever someone new moved in, everyone would go over, bring a cake or something. It wasn't like that in New York. You could live in one of those buildings for years and never get to know a single soul. Once the woman from downstairs rang my bell. She was an old lady, and I thought, Oh good, a friendly neighbor. But all she wanted was to complain about our making noise late at night. I couldn't believe it. We were so quiet, we never had company. I guess she went to bed early, and when Nolan came home from a night game our walking around in the apartment disturbed her.

I couldn't get used to the food shopping, going from one little store to another. I complained so much to Nolan that once he said he'd go along with me to see what all the fuss was about. Well, we went to the dairy store and got these containers of milk, and then we went to the butcher, and the produce store. I warned Nolan not to buy too much because we had to carry everything all the long way home, but he didn't listen. Then one of the containers of milk started leaking, and it was so hot out, and we were dragging all these heavy bundles. Well, when we finally got to our building, climbed up the stairs, and opened the door to the apartment, Nolan just flung those bags of groceries clear across the room. He would never go shopping again.

I pitched in the instructional league in the winter of 1967, and my arm had healed and my velocity was coming back. It looked like I was fully recovered from my first arm injury.

I couldn't believe all the attention I was getting as the 1968 season began. But I guess that's New York City. Tom Seaver had come up to the Mets in 1967 and won the Rookie of the Year Award. The newspapers were comparing me to him. There were also stories comparing me to Sandy Koufax, Bob Gibson, and Bob Feller. That big buildup put pressure on me.

I knew that the Mets had rushed me up from the minors and that I was as raw as anyone who ever came to the big leagues. I didn't have the slightest idea where the ball was going. I was in the big leagues because of my arm, not because I could pitch. It was just as Whitey Herzog had predicted: "It was ironic. The first time I saw Nolan Ryan I knew he had so much ability that he'd be in the majors before he was ready."

I wasn't ready. My idea of pitching was to throw as hard as you could. The Mets had some good young arms, more polished than mine, in Seaver, Jerry Koosman, and Tug McGraw. But I knew I could throw harder than any of them.

My first major league win came in Houston, in a game that was very different from the one in 1966 when I could hardly get anybody out except myself. This time I started off striking out seven of the first ten batters. I was in a great groove and gave up only three hits in six and two-thirds innings before I had to leave because of a bad blister on the middle finger of my pitching hand. We won the game, 4–0, as Danny Frisella pitched the last two innings to preserve my victory.

In my first five starts I struck out forty-four batters in thirty-five innings. On May 14 I set a Met club record for strikeouts in a game—fourteen against the Cincinnati Reds. My record then was 4–2. And there were even more comparisons to Koufax, Gibson, and Feller.

Unfortunately, the blister kept bothering me more and more. Gus Mauch, the trainer, would lance and bandage that finger every day when I was not pitching, but the treatment didn't help much.

Finally Mauch got me a jar of pickle brine from a delicatessen in the Bronx near where he lived. "The brine helps boxers toughen their skin," he told me, "so the stuff should help you, Nolan."

I'd never even eaten a pickle plain, and I bet they taste as bad as the brine smelled. I hated that odor. It got so that I could even smell that brine out on the mound, but I kept soaking my finger in that old jar.

The media was able to get a lot of mileage out of the story, and the Bronx deli didn't do too bad for itself either. It put a huge sign in its window: "Nolan Ryan buys his pickle brine here."

Despite what was written, that brine was no miracle cure; it worked to a point, but a painful callus would still form on the tip of my finger. And there would be blisters under the callus. I finally learned through our new trainer, Tom McKenna, to shave the callus off with a surgical scalpel to where there was nothing left to blister. But I didn't do that until 1970.

In 1968 with the Mets, I had a lot of pain from the blisters and my pitching was affected. After about six or seven innings on the mound my finger would start to blow up and throb.

Gil Hodges, who was in his rookie season as manager of the Mets, believed that starting pitchers should work strictly in turn. However, between my blisters and my Army Reserve duty—which kept me away for weekends—

I missed a lot of turns. There were times that I went almost two weeks without pitching. That inactivity fouled me up because my pitching motion became smoother the more I worked and worse with less activity.

The Mets pitching coach was Rube Walker, a former catcher. He was the type of pitching coach who was excellent with a veteran staff. Walker knew how to get his pitchers in condition but had never pitched himself. I'm sure at times he didn't know what to do with me and my control problems and my being so erratic.

I was really frustrated with the Mets, and Ruth and I were frustrated living in New York. But in a way, playing in New York City was a blessing because we were forced to handle our frustrations at a young age, which helped us later on.

Everything in New York City was such a hassle. Whatever you wanted to do—like taking a drive in a car or playing tennis or getting a table in a restaurant—you always seemed to be dealing with crowds and congestion. And when things were going badly for me at the ballpark, when I was frustrated by not pitching well or not pitching at all, every little thing became magnified.

One of the nice things, though, about being on the Mets was the people who worked at Shea Stadium. They treated everyone really special. It didn't matter to them whether you were a rookie or a ten-year veteran—they treated everyone the same. If there was anything that I needed or Ruth had to have, they would be very helpful and arrange things for us. I always appreciated their kindness.

Another good thing about my being on the Mets was that it brought me together with Tom Seaver. He was the first close friend I had on the Mets. Tom was driven, goal-oriented, polished. He benefited from the fine coaching he had at USC and knew all about pitching and mechanics. I was the opposite, coming out of Texas as a raw talent. Observing him, watching his dedication, his approach to his job, all had a very positive influence on me. He had goals. I had no goals. Tom talked a lot about what he wanted to accomplish in baseball, and it doesn't surprise me to see the kind of career he's had.

TOM SEAVER:

Nolan and I became friends almost immediately. We were both young pitchers, and it was a case of the cows mingling together for a sense of security. Our relationship was strong enough so that we could kid around with each other. We had a stretch where we pitched back to back in the rotation and it was a good run for both of us. I'd win a game and then he'd win. It went on for a bit. Then I had to leave a game trailing 14–7. I was walking up the runway and Nolan was on my tail. "You wimp," he was shouting, "you couldn't even hold a seven-run lead." The next game Nolan pitched, he gave up a big lead. I think he left trailing by eight runs. He made his walk up the runway, and I was right on his tail. I gave him 10 percent more than he had given me the day before. "You big lug," I shouted, "you can't hold a lead no matter how big it is."

You could make a second living back then in New York City going out to talk at banquets or doing personal appear ances, and some of the players did. I wasn't really comfortable doing that, so I didn't usually do any more than I was required to do. But I did get booked into a couple of breakfasts.

I arrived a half hour early for my first breakfast where I was supposed to give a talk. I was pretty hungry and was thinking about sitting down and having a normal breakfast for me—bacon and eggs. I looked around and all that was there was a lot of platters with strange-looking food. I had never seen anything like it. Some of the people that arrived started eating.

"Aren't you hungry?" a man asked.

"I am."

"Then why don't you have something to eat?"

"I will, soon," I said. "Thank you."

The only reason I held back was I wasn't sure what they were eating. It was the first time in my life that I had ever seen lox, bagels, sturgeon, whitefish, herring—the food that was served that morning. When I finally started eating, I enjoyed what I tasted, so things worked out all right. But for a while there I thought I might go hungry. My mom still remembers my calling her one Sunday and saying, "You wouldn't believe what these folks in New York City eat for breakfast!"

RUTH RYAN:

In those days the wives of the players stuck together a lot more than they do today. That was one of the few nice things about living in New York. Older wives would help you find a place to stay, try to help you out if you had any problems. We all tried to live close to Shea Stadium and near each other. That's also changed because today players and their families live quite a distance from the parks they play in.

Nancy Seaver, Tom's wife, was the first person to come up and say hello to me, and we became close friends. LaVonne Koosman, Jerry's wife, was also very nice.

When the team was on the road, all the wives would get together, and the kids would be brought along, too. We'd eat pizzas, visit, and watch the games on TV. There was a sense of camaraderie, of sharing, back then.

Joan Payson, the owner of the Mets, was really nice to all the players' wives. Whenever one of us had a baby, she'd send an engraved silver bowl and spoon from Tiffany's. She seemed to care about the players and their families.

Once during the All-Star break, Nolan and I took a trip to Saratoga, New York, to the horse races and ran into Mrs. Payson there. She invited us into her box to watch the races. Then she announced, "I have an idea. Let's pool our money and make a bet."

Nolan and I were horrified. We had just about fifty dollars between us and that had to last us until we got back to New York City. We were sure Mrs. Payson was a heavy bettor and would expect us to be, too. We were greatly relieved when she asked everyone in her box to contribute one dollar each, and then she gave all the money to her chauffeur to place the bet. I can't remember if we won or lost, but I do remember how glad we were to contribute only one dollar.

Nolan and I always enjoyed being together, and I would

make some of the road trips with him. It really didn't cost any money, and it was good for both of us. After I had made a few of those trips, several of the players on the Mets, older ones, told Nolan that they didn't want me around. They made it seem as if I was invading their privacy. Maybe they were going out with a girlfriend or doing something that they didn't want me to see or know about.

Nolan didn't appreciate what they were telling him. "I'm going to have my wife with me anytime I can," he told them. "I'm not the one that's going to hide from you. If you have to hide—that's your problem."

Although Nolan was very young at the time and they were established major leaguers complaining to him, he didn't back down. He has always had a sense of what's right for him, and he's never been one to be intimidated.

One of my best forms of escape in New York came when games were rained out. Then I'd put on my running shorts and go running in the park with my black Labrador retriever, Molly. We'd run in the quiet rain for forty-five minutes or so, chasing the rabbits that came out of the woods. And the air would be clean and fresh. It was always a peaceful time—good therapy for Molly and me.

Johnny Murphy, who had been a relief pitcher for the Yankees, was then the general manager of the Mets. He didn't seem to have a very high opinion of me. "That Ryan always has some ache or some pain," he told reporters. "You guys call him the myth—and I believe he is one."

I believe it was Murphy who decided to place me on the

disabled list. I missed the whole month of August on account of being placed on the disabled list and the two weeks I spent in summer camp with the Army Reserve.

When I returned to the Mets in September, Hodges stuck me in the bullpen, deep in the bullpen, only calling on me in situations where I had no real chance for a win. My last five decisions were all losses.

I left New York City at the end of the season relieved it was over and anxious to get back home to Alvin. I wanted to go hunting, and I wanted to enjoy time with Ruth with no pressure. Most of all, I wanted to be with Dad. In July he was operated on for a tumor on the lung. Ruth and I had flown home then to be there with him. The doctors had to remove his left lung. We were all stunned. We wanted to stay in Alvin with him, but we had to get back to New York City. Much as we dreaded leaving at such a time, it was all part of the life of a professional baseball player that I was getting used to—the responsibility to be with the team.

In 1968, though, I did have some big moments with the Mets. I struck out the side on nine pitches for the first time in my career on April 19 against Los Angeles. I struck out 133 batters in 134 innings. Only Jerry Koosman and Tom Seaver struck out more. But I appeared in only 21 games, and that was a depressing situation—the blister, the inactivity, the reserve duty, the feeling that I was part of the Mets and at the same time apart from the Mets. Those were discouraging times for a twenty-one-year-old.

The evolution of the 1969 season was very unusual. The Jets had won the Super Bowl in January, but we on the

Mets never thought that was any kind of an omen. In spring training no one thought the Mets would even be in contention.

Then the New York Knicks got everybody excited. For the first time in sixteen years they reached the semifinal round of the play-offs. They went on to win the NBA championship the next year. I was just a kid then who liked basketball, and I watched them play on TV and went with Ruth to a couple of play-off games at Madison Square Garden. That was one of the good things about New York City —there was always some kind of sporting event going on.

The Knicks were an attractive, well-balanced team with good playmakers and an excellent supporting cast. They were an exciting team to watch. I especially liked Willis Reed, who represented a lot of power at the center position. And I was a Bill Bradley fan. His style was constant. Bradley never said much but gave the team the same maximum effort in each game he played. He was a true professional. The Knick coach, Red Holzman, kept in the background and never seemed to intrude on the way the Knicks played the game, but he always had them playing team basketball, and that was something I could appreciate.

The New York Mets began the 1969 season as a 100–1 shot to win the National League pennant. Our opening day lineup didn't figure to scare anyone: Tommie Agee in center field, Rod Gaspar in right field, Ken Boswell at second base, Cleon Jones in left field, Ed Charles at third base, Ed Kranepool at first. Jerry Grote was the catcher, Bud Harrelson played shortstop, and Tom Seaver pitched.

It's incredible that the Mets even contended for the pennant because the Cubs had a much better team. Chicago had a club of veterans, with stars like Ernie Banks, Ron Santo, and Billy Williams. The Cubs, managed by Leo Durocher, staked a claim to first place right from the start of the season and most everyone thought they had the division title wrapped up.

We kind of sneaked up on them into second place, after a while, winning eleven straight games. No one took us seriously as a threat—we didn't even take ourselves seriously. Gil Hodges kept saying that we couldn't be considered contenders until we reached .500.

On May 21 in Atlanta, Tom Seaver beat the Braves 3–0 to bring our team record to 18–18. Players who had been with the Mets awhile, like Ed Kranepool, were really excited. They wanted to break out some champagne. But Tom Seaver would have none of it.

"What's so good about .500?" he said. "That's just mediocre. I'm a bit tired of hearing the jokes about the old Mets. Let Rod Kanehl and Marvelous Marv laugh about the old Mets. . . . You know when we will drink the champagne? When we win the pennant."

The players on the Cubs and the Mets did not like each other, to put it mildly. All through that season there were incidents. In May there were exchanges of beanballs. Seaver had knocked down Ron Santo with a pitch. Then when Tom came up to bat he was hit in the back by a pitch from Bill Hands. Seaver was a pleasant guy, but he was also a fierce competitor. The next inning he plunked Hands in the stomach with one of his pitches. That created a bad scene, and the umpires were hard pressed to prevent a riot.

On August 13 we were 9$1/2$ games back of the Cubs and then it all turned around. We won 38 of our last 49 to overtake Chicago.

Pitching did it for us. Only twice in those last 49 games did we score as many as 8 runs in a game, but Seaver and Koosman and some of the others were on their game. Tom won 10 in a row from August 9 on and finished the year with a 25–7 record. There were 28 shutouts by the Met pitching staff that season, four shy of the all-time record set by the 1907 and 1909 Chicago Cubs.

On September 10 I was given one of my rare starts. I went the distance, striking out eleven and giving up just three hits as we beat Montreal, 7–1. That was a satisfying moment for me because it gave us a one-game lead over the Cubs, and the applications for tickets for the World Series started coming in.

It was called the "Year of the Amazin' Mets" and for good reason. On September 15 I sat and watched as Steve Carlton set a modern major league nine-inning-game strikeout record, fanning nineteen Mets, only to lose that game to us 4–3. Ron Swoboda got Carlton for two two-run homers.

Being there on the New York Mets through all the excitement—the tension of that pennant race; the come-from-behind wins; the media hype; big crowds wherever our team went; the noise, especially from our very loyal fans at Shea Stadium and from the Bleacher Bums at Wrigley

Field in Chicago—that was an experience. Looking back now, I guess I should have enjoyed it all more.

The year 1969 was also another tough one at home. My mother suffered a stroke and had to have surgery. I yearned to be home to help out my parents, and I was feeling rather depressed about my overall situation.

But New York Met fans were anything but depressed that year, especially on September 24, 1969. After Gary Gentry pitched a four-hit shutout over the St. Louis Cardinals to clinch our National League East title, it seemed that everyone of the 54,928 fans in attendance for that game charged out onto the playing field.

All the bases were dug up. Home plate disappeared. Sod was removed. The security force at Shea had been reinforced for that game, but they couldn't control those people, who just ran amuck. It was fortunate that game was our last of the regular season at Shea because it took the groundskeepers several days to get the field back into any kind of shape.

In our clubhouse the celebration wasn't too shabby either. Champagne, beer, soda, shaving cream—whatever could be sprayed or poured was in use.

It was an outstanding moment in the history of the New York Mets and for all of us who were on that team. I looked around at my teammates—Seaver, Koosman, McGraw, Grote, and the others—and at that moment I did feel a pride in being part of it all, part of the team.

The Atlanta Braves were our competition in the best of five National League play-offs. They had some tough hitters on that club—Rico Carty, Hank Aaron, Orlando Cepeda. A five-run eighth gave us a win in the first game. Tug McGraw came in to save the 11–6 second-game victory. I watched both games from the bullpen in Atlanta. Although Hodges had needed relievers in those first two games, he didn't call on me.

We went for the sweep in the third game at Shea Stadium before more than fifty thousand roaring fans. Gary Gentry started for us against Pat Jarvis, the guy who was my first major league strikeout.

Gentry gave up a two-run homer to Hank Aaron in the first inning and got into more trouble in the third. There were two Braves on base and no outs. I got the call to come in from the bullpen. Coming in there in such a big game with my history of control problems with runners on base, I was truly surprised. I guess Hodges thought it was too early to use a short reliever like Tug McGraw or Ron Taylor, so he went for me.

Hodges gave me the ball and said, "Keep the ball down."

That was all he said to me. I stood out on the mound aware that every move of mine was being watched by a national TV audience and all those people at Shea Stadium. Throwing my warm-up pitches, I was wild and scared and wondered if I would be able to get away without walking anyone. Plus I was concerned about making a mistake with a bad pitch or throwing a wild pitch.

Rico Carty, a .340 hitter that 1969 season, had a one-ball

and two-strike count on him left over from Gentry. I threw
Rico a low and away fastball. Carty just stood there—frozen
—and the ump called "Strike three!" Hodges sent out the
sign for me to walk Orlando Cepeda. I wasn't too happy
about that. The bases were now loaded. I knew a walk or a
wild pitch would cost us a run. I bore down. I got Clete
Boyer on a strikeout and Bob Didier on a pop-up. It felt
good to get off that mound and into the dugout. The fans
gave me a standing ovation, and many of my teammates
came over and congratulated me.

In the fifth inning I made the mistake of an inexperienced pitcher. After fouling off three fastballs away—one
too many—Cepeda clubbed a two-run homer to give them
a 4–3 lead. I didn't make any other mistakes and pitched
shutout baseball the rest of the way, and we rallied and
wound up winning 7–4.

In my seven innings of pitching I gave up just three hits
and two runs to get the win that sent us into the World
Series against Baltimore. Most of the '69 season I was kind
of like the forgotten man on the Mets, but in the clubhouse
that afternoon I felt like part of the team again. The champagne and the shouts and the media attention still remain
with me. It was the high moment of my career to that
point. There had been pressure, but I had handled it.

"Do you think you will get a start in the World Series?" a
reporter asked.

"I don't know about that," I told him. "But I know I was
throwing good out there against the Braves and I know I

can do the same again. I do hope to get more of a chance to pitch."

There were stories in the newspapers that speculated about my getting a World Series start. Gil had his starting rotation set, and it didn't include me. When the series got under way, I was back in my old position in the bullpen.

Baltimore was a tough, experienced team and was heavily favored to win the World Series. It was a club built by Frank Cashen, today the general manager of the Mets. The Orioles had stars like Davey Johnson (now the manager of the Mets) at second base, Frank Robinson, Brooks Robinson, Paul Blair, and Boog Powell. Three Baltimore starters —Jim Palmer, Dave McNally, and Mike Cuellar—won fifty-nine games between them during the season.

"We're here," Brooks Robinson said, "to prove there are no miracles." And Frank Robinson was quoted as saying, "Bring on Ron Gaspar!" He purposely mixed up the names of Rod Gaspar and Ron Swoboda. That was his way of giving us the needle.

Prior to the first game of the series we had a team meeting to go over their hitters. The report was practically the same on each one of them: "Good fastball hitter. Don't give him a fastball to hit."

Finally one of our players asked, "What the hell are we supposed to throw?" We were a pitching staff of hard throwers.

On the first pitch of the first game Don Buford hit Tom Seaver's fastball into our bullpen for a home run. I remember thinking how correct that scouting report was.

We split the first two games with them, getting good pitching performances from Seaver and Koosman. The third game was played before 56,335 fans at Shea, and it seemed everyone of them was shouting, "Let's go, Mets! Let's go, Mets!"

Gentry had allowed just three hits and led 4–0 going into the seventh, but he had pitched in and out of trouble all game long. Suddenly he lost all control and, with two outs, walked the bases full.

Hodges waved me in from the bullpen. "Get the ball over," he said. "And make sure you keep it down." Again nervousness mixed with desire to do well as I took my warm-ups.

Paul Blair was the Baltimore batter, a good hitter, a selective hitter. I didn't waste any time out there. I threw as hard as I could and kept the ball low and got him in a hole with two quick strikes.

Blair was digging in, and I guess I should have brushed him back or wasted a pitch, but I was anxious to get out of the inning. I wound and threw a fastball up and over the plate. Blair made contact. The instant the ball left his bat I knew it was trouble. I turned, and the ball was headed to the warning track in right center—extra bases, I thought. Tommie Agee, who had made a tremendous catch earlier in the game, kept running to his left and toward the fence. I guessed he had no chance to catch the ball even if he reached it. He reached the ball just as it was about to hit the edge of the dirt on the warning track. Diving, skidding on one knee, Agee gloved the ball just inches off the ground.

Three outs! Blair was at second base when Agee caught the ball, and he might have had a shot at an inside-the-park home run.

It was an amazing catch, a catch that sent a charge through all the fans at Shea; I felt like applauding, too. Agee had gotten me off the hook, and I gotten away with a bad pitch.

I went into the ninth with a 5–0 lead and retired the first two batters on fly balls. Then I got too fine and walked Mark Belanger on a 3–2 count. Clay Dalrymple reached base on a liner to second that Al Weis knocked down but couldn't make a throw on. I loaded the bases by walking Don Buford.

Paul Blair was the next batter. I could see the Orioles bench was sensing the kill, and Gil Hodges could see that, too. He came out to the mound.

"You got anything left?" he asked.

"Yes, sir," I said.

Hodges let me stay in. In the past Hodges had not even spoken to me in the same kind of circumstances. He'd simply come out and get the ball and take me out.

I reached back and threw two fastballs past Blair for strikes. The situation was the same as the first time I faced him in the game. I wasn't going to make the same mistake twice.

I went into my windup and threw probably as good a curveball as I have ever thrown. Blair flinched a bit in surprise and took the pitch for strike three. I was credited with the save, and we took a 2–1 lead in the series.

We won the next game in ten innings behind Tom Seaver. And a 5–3 win in the fifth game brought the Mets their first World Championship.

When that final game ended, Shea Stadium was like a battle zone—just the way it had been when we clinched the division. Players were running for cover, happy to get off the field with their uniforms still on. People were scratching and clawing for souvenirs. Turf was dug up. Bases were pulled out. People milled about in the stadium for what seemed like hours. In our clubhouse the celebrating went on for some time, too. Casey Stengel was there and he was especially excited about the World Championship. I guess he never forgot how bad those early Met clubs were.

It was an amazing time. Mother and Dad were doing fine, and I had flown them up to stay with us in New York for the Series. Things were happening so fast. We were suddenly the toast of the town. Tickertape parades, banquets, media attention, the whole thing. You almost got to the point where you were taking all of it for granted.

I knew I had contributed a bit to the team's success. The World Series had helped restore some of my confidence in my ability and my desire to play. Yet I still felt like a guy on the outside looking in. My role on the Mets was unclear. And I was still very concerned about what the future would bring.

RUTH RYAN:

After the World Championship, there were all kinds of attentions lavished on the Met players, all kinds of deals available. Comedian Phil Foster organized a nightclub act in Las Vegas for some of the players where they would sing, dance in a chorus line, and tell jokes. Nolan was asked to go with them. We were promised a free trip, all expenses paid plus $10,000, which was a lot of money for us back then. I kind of liked the idea of going to Las Vegas, seeing all the shows, going to all those nice restaurants. But Nolan turned it down.

"I'm not an entertainer, Ruth," he told me. "I just wouldn't feel right getting up there in front of all those people doing something I don't know how to do."

So that was it. I never tried to encourage him to do something he wasn't comfortable about.

A cruise company also invited some of the players and their wives to come along on a cruise free of charge. And again Nolan didn't want to go. He was in a big hurry to get back to Alvin. Later we found out that the players who went were disappointed with the experience. They were expected to be on hand, kind of an attraction for the paying travelers. So Nolan was right after all. Those two events showed me, early on in Nolan's career, that he couldn't be persuaded to do what he felt wasn't right for him. I was impressed by the way he was able to handle the pressures of playing in New York when he was still such a young man.

"This will be an important spring for Nolan," Gil Hodges told reporters in March of 1970. "He's now on the threshold of becoming not only a good pitcher but a great one. He has a fastball that I rank with Sandy Koufax's, a curve that gets even sharper, and an improving changeup. What's more, he's been through enough in the last few years to have gained experience, not only getting into tough situations, but getting out of them as well."

When I read those words of Hodges in the newspapers, I felt like he was giving me a vote of confidence. And I got off to an excellent beginning in 1970. In my first start, I one-hit the Phillies and struck out fifteen. That was the Met club record for strikeouts in a single game. However, I held that record for only four days. Tom Seaver broke it by getting nineteen strikeouts against San Diego.

My inconsistency was bothering me again. I gave up only five hits in my first three starts and then lost my rhythm. I would have a good game and then fall apart, unable to get the ball over the plate. I had eleven strikeouts in five innings against Houston—and then my control left me and I was all over the place.

My Army Reserve duty on weekends and two weeks in summer camp set me back even more. There were days in Houston, Fort Leonard Wood in Missouri, Fort Hood in Texas, and Mobile, Alabama—in and out of duffel bags and suitcases, one day in a baseball uniform, the next day in an Army uniform. My reserve unit was upgraded to a top priority, so we had duty every other weekend in Houston.

Hodges kept to his philosophy of working pitchers strictly in turn in the rotation. And my shuffling back and forth from the reserves to the Mets caused me sometimes to have ten or twelve days between starts. Once I started after an eighteen-day break. That was no way for me to have my rhythm. With fewer and fewer starts, the pressure on me to produce became even greater.

That summer my dad passed away. It was like a great oak tree had fallen. His death was a terrible blow to me and put lots of things in perspective, and I started to think about what I was doing with my own life.

Flying back to New York City with Ruth after the funeral, I said, "Maybe I ought to hang it up, quit the game. I'm twenty-three, but I feel ten years older. I've been in baseball for six years now and I haven't really gotten anywhere."

"You're in the major leagues, Nolan," she said, "and you've had some big games."

"Not enough," I said. "And I've had some bad games. I just don't know if the effort is worth it."

"Do you think you can still succeed?"

"Sure, Ruth," I said, "but I don't know if it's worth it, worth the price we are both paying. I'm not enjoying it. Do you like the baseball life?"

"Not that much, Nolan. But we have to give it a chance. If you were doing better, things would be better. You don't want to quit now and wonder later what might have been. Let's stay with the game a little longer and see if things get better."

Things started out all right for me in 1971. I was in the regular rotation, pitched a couple of shutouts and several one-run games, struck out sixteen against San Diego. My record was 8–4 by the end of June, but as the season progressed, my performance regressed. As I look back on it now, I think being in New York and not being as dedicated as I would later become played a big factor in my second-half slump. I was not cut out to be a New Yorker.

Johnny Murphy had died, and Bob Scheffing, a former catcher, had replaced him as general manager of the Mets. One night we flew back to New York City after a road trip. It was pretty late, and Scheffing, who lived close to my home in Bayside, gave me a ride home in his car.

We got to talking about my situation on the Mets. He was the kind of man you could talk to, much more understanding than Murphy had been.

"You know," I began, "I'm not that happy with the way I'm pitching and the ways things are going. I'm just flat out frustrated."

"You've made that very clear to everyone, Nolan."

"Then under the circumstances," I said, "maybe it would be best for all of us that you trade me if the opportunity arises. It would give me a new start and maybe you can get something you need."

"Trades aren't the easiest thing to manage," Scheffing said, "but if you are that unhappy, we'll see what we can do."

When the 1971 season finally came to an end, disappointment existed all the way around. The Mets finished in fourth place. And I wound up with a record of 10–14, completing just 3 of 26 starts.

I decided to drive home after the final game of the season. Ruth was seven and a half months pregnant, and I couldn't wait to head home to Alvin with her.

When I came back to our apartment in Bayside, Queens, after the final game at Shea, all of our belongings were packed up ready for the trip. Ruth said, "Let's get a good night's sleep so we can get a fresh start in the morning."

"No," I said, "I'm really anxious to get home. We're gonna get in the car right now, Ruth. I know we won't be coming back here. So this will be our last trip from this place."

I was glad to be heading home. I thought about what my future might have in store for us. Now Ruth was pregnant with our first child, and I was excited about that. At the same time I was despondent about what I thought was another lost year. Yet somehow I had gained confidence in my ability and was determined to prove that I could pitch successfully in the major leagues.

"We won't be coming back to the Mets," I told her. "I think they'll trade me, but I also know I can pitch and would like to start new with another organization."

"What if they don't trade you, Nolan? You aren't still thinking of quitting baseball?"

"I don't know, Ruth," I said. I really didn't know. "I'll cross that bridge when I come to it, but I think Scheffing will honor my request and trade me."

Our son Reid was born in Houston on November 21,

1971. Two weeks later, I was headed out the door to class at Alvin Junior College when the phone rang. Just that morning I had commented to Ruth that it was the final day of the baseball winter meetings. "If the Mets are going to trade me," I told her, "today will be the day."

Ruth answered the phone and put me on to speak to Bob Scheffing. "Nolan," he said, "you're going to sunny California." I instantly thought he meant the Los Angeles Dodgers. Then when he told me I had been traded to the California Angels, I was in shock. I had just assumed I would always be a National Leaguer. The only thing I knew about the Angels were all the problems they had that year with Alex Johnson and with the gun in the clubhouse. Even then I wanted to play for Houston because it was home. The American League and the California Angels seemed like a million miles away. I didn't know anybody out there. It really was like starting all over again.

The Mets made a deal hoping to solve their third-base problems. A lot of people say it was the worst trade they ever made. They traded me, outfielder Lee Stanton, and a couple of other young players for Jim Fregosi, who was a veteran player. I read that Gil Hodges approved the deal, that he wanted Jim Fregosi, and that he thought I was the starting pitcher he would miss the least.

PART III

CALIFORNIA

Going to the California Angels was a fresh start for me, and my experience there would totally turn around my career. The encouraging thing about it all was that I was made to feel wanted right from the beginning.

After the trade was announced, Harry Dalton called. He had recently come over from Baltimore to be the general manager of the Angels.

"Welcome aboard, Nolan," he said. "We're glad to have you with the Angels. You're the main part of my first trade and I want it to be a good one. You can be a big star with California, and we're going to give you every chance to be one. Here you will get a chance to pitch."

I thanked him for his encouraging words, for the salary increase he gave me of three thousand dollars, for his kindness in offering assistance in getting Ruth, my infant son, Reid, and me settled in California. And through that winter my thoughts about making good with the Angels became an all-consuming passion.

New York City was thousands of miles away. My military obligations were finished. I was anxious to go to spring training in 1972 and meet my new teammates and see how I could do in a new league.

Spring training opened with the Angels in the desert town of Holtville, California, at the minor league complex of the team. The only player I knew there was Lee Stanton, who I had played with in the minor leagues and in a few games with the Mets in 1970–71. He had come over with me in the trade to the Angels.

My first day in camp was quite an experience. I was standing around in the infield when an older man, who seemed to be one of the California coaches, hollered to me, "Get out in the infield. Get some practice."

He then started to hit ground balls to me, one after another. He hit balls to my left, to my right, to my left. After about ten minutes of that, I was thinking that I'd had enough. But he just kept on hitting those grounders one after another. After twenty minutes of that treatment I thought I was going to throw up. One more ground ball would have done it.

That was my first encounter with Jimmie Reese, a former player, who had been Babe Ruth's roommate for a time. Jimmie would have as much to do with my success in baseball as anyone. He would become a special friend, a confidant, a coach who always kept me in shape by hitting fungoes and grounders to me. He is one of those people for whom baseball is a way of life.

I was rescued that day at Holtville from Jimmie Reese's ground-ball workout by Tom Morgan, the pitching coach.

"Hey, Nolan," he called out, "come over here and start warming up. You're going to throw some batting practice."

I did what Tom told me to do. Anything, I thought, was better than the ground-ball routine. However, when I first started throwing the ball I thought I was going to die.

"That Reese gave you the treatment." Tom laughed. "He's a good guy, though. Next time when you've had enough just tell him. Sometimes he gets a little carried away with enthusiasm."

It was also at Holtville that I first began to work with Jeff Torborg, a highly intelligent player, a catcher who had worked with Sandy Koufax and Don Drysdale. It was a fortunate thing for me linking up with Jeff. In the very first workout he noticed some things about my pitching that no one had ever told me about.

"You're overthrowing," Jeff told me, "and you're rushing your motion. You don't have to labor so hard to get the ball up to the plate."

"I've always worked hard to get the ball up there," I told him. "I thought that was what helped account for my speed."

"No, Nolan," he said. "When you rush your motion and you stride out too soon, your arm can't catch up and the ball gets released too soon. That's why when you're wild, you're not wild from side to side but wild high."

Torborg and I worked a lot together. What he said made sense. I knew what I had to do, but it was a little like learning to pitch all over again. Sometimes only one of fifteen pitches that I threw to him I threw properly. I knew it would take a lot of hard work to get what he said right.

JEFF TORBORG:

I know that it was a very frustrating time for Nolan, a new ball club, a new league, and he was struggling with his mechanics. We had a few disagreements, a few battles. But Nolan had so much drive and was such a willing worker. He worked as hard as any human being could. The problem with Nolan was that he worked so hard he almost got sick. We even had a few arguments when I tried to get him to ease off.

The most impressive thing about Nolan was that he was not a bewildered kid but a guy who knew his own mind. He knew what he wanted to do. We just didn't know the right route to get there, but he was willing to work very hard to find it.

Another important influence on my pitching was Tom Morgan. He began his career with the Yankees and finished it up with the Angels and became their pitching coach.

Tom knew all about pitching deliveries. He didn't attempt to change mine radically, but he did alter it for the better. My whole motion became tighter, more compact, more conservative, better suited to throwing strikes. My natural motion remained, but Tom put it into more of a rhythm, slowed it down. There were times when I had it all going—a comfortable feeling, the natural and fluid motion. But those times came and went.

After two weeks in Holtville, we broke camp for Palm Springs, where the spring headquarters were. This was my

· 7 6 ·

opportunity to make the starting rotation and, I hoped, make a good impression. What a disaster it all turned into.

I was wilder than I had ever been. The harder I tried, the wilder I became. My old thoughts of quitting baseball started creeping back into my mind.

By the end of spring training things were a real mess. There was a baseball strike on. I was not so concerned about the strike and its issues as much as I was about my own personal problems. I was a young player not yet established, mainly concerned about my future in baseball. I felt I had blown my new start with the horrendous spring I had. I was coming to the conclusion that I wasn't cut out for the baseball line of work, and I was yearning to rid myself of all the frustration and anxiety I was experiencing.

Then a new problem developed. Ruth and I had a rented house in Anaheim. We had no money coming in because of the strike. This predicament further fueled my thoughts of quitting. I discussed this once again with Ruth, and again she convinced me to stick it out. I wound up having to borrow money from a bank in Alvin and put up as collateral the money I was set to receive on my 1971 income tax return.

RUTH RYAN:

We had hardly any money and they discouraged families from staying with their husbands. That made it hard on us at the time. The only way we could afford to be together was by borrowing a trailer from Nolan's sister, a little camper-trailer, and we parked it in a KOA campground, and that's how we lived with the baby for about three weeks. It was hot in the daytime and freezing cold at night. But at least we were together.

At the Palm Springs training camp, where the Angels stayed after leaving Holtville, they wouldn't let wives stay in the same hotel. So we rented a house in Anaheim then that we planned to live in during the season. And Nolan drove back and forth to Palm Springs for his workouts. It was a long, hard drive in his little Volkswagen. He'd get up really early in the morning and drive and come home at night.

We had to borrow money to get to California, and no salary came in during the strike. We had the baby and the debts and we were nearly broke. Nolan felt close to quitting and going back to Texas. That was a rough spring.

The New York media criticized the Mets for trading me to the Angels, and the California press thought Harry Dalton was a fool for getting me. The Angels had three good pitchers—Clyde Wright, Rudy May, and Andy Messersmith. Fregosi had been a popular player, and the reporters said the Angels should have acquired a proven hitter for him, not an unproven pitcher like me.

I was discouraged by my poor showing and the criticism of the trade in the press. If Ruth had not convinced me to stay on, I would have quit on the spot. As it turned out, she and the people on the Angels had a whole lot more confidence in my abilities at that time than I did.

Del Rice was the rookie manager of the Angels, and he was on a spot himself. He had a one-year contract and a ball club that was kind of patchwork and didn't have that much talent. That 1972 California team wound up with an outfield of Vada Pinson, Lee Stanton, and Ken Berry. Bob Oliver was the first baseman, Sandy Alomar played second base, the shortstop was Leo Cardenas, and Ken McMullen was the third baseman. Jeff Torborg split the catching with Art Kusnyer.

Art was my roommate that first year and became a close friend. I always have to laugh to myself about my first encounter with him. At Holtville we worked out as two squads, so I never saw a lot of the guys on the Angels during the workouts. About a week after we had been in camp, we had an intersquad game, and I was scheduled to pitch two innings. I came out to pitch in the fifth inning. Art was the catcher. I had no idea who he was. During my warm-up pitches, he ran out to the mound to get our signs straight. "Hey, Huck-face," he said, "what signs are you using?"

I couldn't believe he was talking to me. I started looking around to see who he was talking to. That was my introduction to the most enjoyable roommate I ever had in baseball —the man who called me "Huck-face."

Even though Del Rice had his hands full, he was always encouraging me. "Don't worry about what the newspapers say," he told me, "and don't worry about how you did this spring. It's only spring training. I'm planning on your being one of my starters. I know you're going to do all right."

The confidence that Del Rice and Harry Dalton and the others associated with the Angels showed in me gave me the lift I needed. I was surprised that they let me start the third game of the season. It was against Minnesota, and I beat the Twins, 2–0. I felt good about that. I knew I had found something. Then I lost it. Texas beat me, Baltimore racked me. By the middle of May my record was 2–4.

The Angels were doing poorly, and I wasn't helping matters much. Rice was starting to lose patience, and he was a patient man. He had spoken to me more in the first part of that season than Hodges had spoken to me all the time I was with the Mets.

"I'm going to have to put you in the bullpen, Nolan," Rice said. "Maybe you'll come around there. I just can't go with you as a starter anymore. I can't afford it the way the team is going."

"Whatever you say, Del," I told him. I never argued with a manager, and I wasn't doing him or the team any good at that point as a starter.

Tom Morgan was listening to our conversation and now he cut in. "Del, I do think that Nolan is close to turning the corner."

"How's that?" Rice asked.

"Well, Nolan had some big moments and then he just lost it. All he needs is more work. I'll put the time in with him between starts and on our off days. Let's just keep him in the starting rotation a little longer. I'm sure it will work out."

Rice agreed. And Morgan, Torborg, Art Kusnyer, and even Angel coach John Roseboro, a former catcher, all worked with me.

Pitch after pitch, day after day, I was throwing to

My mom and dad—they were
a handsome couple. (PHOTO
COURTESY NOLAN RYAN)

Class photo, 1955–56 Alvin
Elementary School. (PHOTO
COURTESY NOLAN RYAN)

Little League days—one of
the happiest times of my life.
(PHOTO COURTESY NOLAN RYAN)

The Alvin High School pitcher,
1965. (PHOTO COURTESY
NOLAN RYAN)

Marrying Ruth on June 26, 1967, was one of the best things I ever did in my life.

Early years with the Mets: Jerry Grote, center, and Bud Harrelson, right. (PHOTO COURTESY NOLAN RYAN)

Gil Hodges, left, Rube Walker, and Gary Gentry, right— congratulations all around. (PHOTO COURTESY NOLAN RYAN)

Shea Stadium, 1969: posing during Family Day. (PHOTO COURTESY NOLAN RYAN)

1969—the Mets—victory over the Braves in the play-offs. (PHOTO COURTESY NOLAN RYAN)

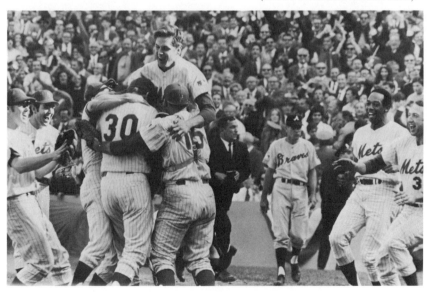

Publicity shot—during my time with the Mets. (PHOTO COURTESY NOLAN RYAN)

Ruth and Reid flanked by a couple of fans—the guy on the left came over from Disneyland. (PHOTO COURTESY NOLAN RYAN)

always love being around animals. (PHOTO COURTESY NOLAN RYAN)

Hunting and enjoying the great outdoors during the off-season. (PHOTO COURTESY NOLAN RYAN)

Publicity shot from my time with the Angels. (PHOTO COURTESY NOLAN RYAN)

Torborg, to Kusnyer, to Roseboro. Tom Morgan was always there, watching, getting me in a groove. It was exhausting work, mechanical work, boring at times, but those days turned around my career. To accomplish anything in life you need faith and you sometimes need help. I was getting the help from those guys on the Angels, and I will always be in debt to them for caring for a young, wild-armed pitcher. I got the faith from the help they gave me, and then it all suddenly started to pay off.

I pitched a shutout against the White Sox. I went against the Tigers and three-hit them, but lost the game. I got a two-hitter against Oakland. I was in a groove, pitching every fourth day. With the regular work, my curveball was getting better and my change-up was improving.

By the middle of the season I had won ten games, but our team was slipping further and further out of pennant contention. Our hitting was pretty bad and the pitching, aside from Clyde Wright and myself, was struggling.

On July 9 I pitched the best game of my career to that point. I struck out sixteen against Boston, eight of them in a row. Those eight straight strikeouts set an American League record. In one inning I had things going so well that I struck out the side on nine pitches to become the only one to do that in both leagues. I wound up with a one-hitter. I walked Tommy Harper to start the game, struck out the second hitter, and then Carl Yastrzemski hit a curve through the hole between third and short. I finished up by retiring the next twenty-six batters for the win.

On the field, things were going well. Off the field, things

were much better than they had been in New York City. Ruth, Reid, and I were comfortable in a split-level house in Anaheim. We had a swimming pool and a patio with a barbecue. Coming from Texas, I always liked to barbecue. The environment was peaceful, and we had nice neighbors. The house was just about a ten-minute drive from the ballpark, and if we drove another ten minutes we were able to be close to the desert and the mountains. It wasn't Alvin, but it was a pretty good substitute—an unpressured Southern California life-style.

When I was with the Mets, the movie *Von Ryan's Express* was a recent big hit. The newspapers started to refer to me as "the Ryan Express." I was flattered by the nickname then. Now, in California, I was even more flattered by what the opposition was saying about me.

DICK WILLIAMS:

I faced Sandy Koufax in intrasquad games when we were teammates on the Dodgers. I always thought he was the fastest pitcher I'd ever seen—a lightning bolt. But Nolan was even faster. He threw a heavy ball. That was heavy speed. You couldn't look for his breaking ball. Even his change of pace, at eighty-five miles per hour, was faster than most other pitchers' fastballs. They say Nolan used to stick out his tongue when he threw a breaking ball. No one ever looked at his tongue— there just wasn't enough time.

When I managed those World Championship teams at Oakland with all those fine hitters, our fellows feared facing Nolan

Ryan. He didn't throw at anybody, but he was conveniently wild. His ball just took off.

PHIL GARNER:

With Oakland, I faced Nolan in a game where he had a no-hitter going. I came to bat with two men on base. He had walked a guy and hit a guy. Nolan had two strikes on me that he got with his mighty fastball and then he threw a curveball down and away. I hit it off the wall for a double. The newspaper headlines the next day read: ".246 Hitter One-Hits Ryan and Beats Him, 2–1."

So I was feeling pretty cocky about facing him going into a game the last half of that season. But he was unhittable that night, striking out sixteen or seventeen batters. If you touched the ball it was by mere mistake.

My first two times up, he struck me out on six pitches—low and away fastballs. My third time up, the first two pitches again were low and away fastballs for strikes. I decided not to get caught again with a low and away fastball. I leaned out over the plate hoping to just peck the ball. In a flash in that thousandth of a second I saw his fastball thrown as hard as he could throw it coming right behind my ear. My whole life passed before me. I tried to dig a hole beneath the batter's box 'cause I was scared to death. As he was winding up to throw his next pitch, I was already walking to the dugout. It was strike three for me, and I was just happy to be out of there.

DICK WILLIAMS:

> One game Reggie Jackson hit a line drive off Nolan that was caught by the center fielder. As Reggie made his turn around first base and headed to the bench he cut across the mound and gave Nolan a good-natured pat on the fanny. The next four or five games when he faced Reggie, Nolan was conveniently wild. That was the last time Reggie ever did that fanny pat to any pitcher.

REGGIE JACKSON:

> Ryan's the only guy who put fear in me. Not because he could get me out but because he could kill me. Every hitter likes fastballs like everybody likes ice cream. But you don't like it when someone's stuffing it into you by the gallon. That's how you felt when Nolan was throwing fastballs by you. You just hoped to mix in a walk so you could have a good night and go 0 for 3.

I much preferred to pitch to people like Reggie, who went on to strike out more times than anybody in baseball history. I got more than my share of his total. I always knew Reggie was going to strike out a lot against me. He was the kind of hitter who would not give in to you because he swung hard with the intent of hitting a home run. A Reggie type of hitter was always one who if I made my pitch I would strike him out or get him out. And if I made a mistake, then I would get hurt. It was always a challenge to face Reggie.

I did get hurt in a couple of games before the 1972 All-Star Game. One of those games was against the Yankees at the Stadium, and a New York writer said: "That's the same old Nolan Ryan—he's in an Angel uniform but he pitches the same way he did on the Mets." That burned me up.

I made the All-Star team for the first time in my career, and it was a thrill to be there in Atlanta with all those top players. I felt my hard work was starting to pay off.

The Angels finished in fifth place in our division in 1972. We were a struggling, building ball club that wound up eighteen games behind Oakland. I tried to do my part to keep us winning, but it was a tough deal. I led the American League in strikeouts with 329—the fourth-best total ever at that time. I pitched 9 shutouts to lead the league. I should have pitched more because many times it was either I pitched a shutout or I lost. More than half a dozen of my losses in 1972 were 1–0, 2–0, 2–1.

In my final start of the season against Oakland, going for my twentieth win, I lost the game, 2–1, when Campy Campaneris stole second base and then scored. I wound up the year giving up the fewest hits of all American League pitchers per 9 innings, an overall record of 19–16, and a 2.28 ERA.

The patience and the help the Angel organization extended enabled me to have a tremendous year. I was finally learning to pitch with more than my arm. Although I knew I could still improve—I led the league in walks, hit batsmen, and wild pitches—I could feel I was heading in the right direction. I guess the Angel management could, too. My salary for 1973 was raised to $54,000—almost twice what I had earned in my first year in Anaheim. And for the first time in my life I looked forward to a new baseball season with very high hopes and lots of confidence. I never dreamed, however, that I would pitch two no-hitters and set the all-time single season strikeout record.

My first no-hitter was against the Royals in Kansas City in a night game on May 15, 1973. I had been knocked out in my start before that, and, warming up before the game, I wasn't too happy with my stuff. I didn't seem to have good velocity. I thought I'd have to pitch to spots, move the ball around, and avoid walks—and then maybe I'd have a better chance to win the game.

In the early innings I gave up a couple of walks and had to strike John Mayberry out to get out of trouble. By the sixth inning we had a 3–0 lead, and I was given a lot of breathing space in the dugout. The guys on the Angels were caught up in the old baseball superstition: don't bother a pitcher going for a no-hitter. Don't even talk to him. The longer the game goes, the farther away they sit from him, as if he's got the plague or something.

I actually like that treatment because whenever I'm pitching I don't like to mix with others. Talking distracts me. I like to be focused on the job at hand and concentrate on what I'm going to do the next inning. There were only about twelve thousand fans at Royals Stadium that night, but I didn't notice the crowd anyway.

As I took the mound for my warm-up pitches to Jeff Torborg in the bottom of the eighth inning, I wanted that no-hitter. I knew that the game was being televised back to Southern California and that Ruth was watching it in Anaheim. I knew I needed to get ahead of the hitter in the count so I wouldn't have to give him anything to hit.

With one out in the eighth, pinch hitter Gail Hopkins looped a ball into left field. Rudy Meoli raced back from his shortstop position. I thought the ball was going to drop. At the last instant, Rudy made a running, over-the-shoulder catch with his back to the plate. Hopkins was out. I got the next batter, and the game moved into the ninth.

Sitting alone in the dugout while my teammates batted in the top of the ninth inning, I felt a lot of anxiety. I was thinking about the batters I would be facing and what I would throw them. I was concerned about making a mistake.

Speedy Freddie Patek led off for K.C. in the bottom of the ninth. He had a small strike zone and was a good bunter. Patek went for my first pitch—a high fastball—and popped it up to first. Steve Hovley was next. He ran the count to 2–2 and then swung hard at a fastball and came up empty.

The last batter I had to get out was Amos Otis, who had been my teammate on the Mets. His last time up, Otis had grounded out hard on a curveball. I decided all I'd give him this time was heat. He swung and missed the first fastball I threw him. Then he tagged the next one, but I knew the second it left his bat that it was in the air and that it was catchable. Ken Berry, who had come into the game for defense, had to run all the way to the warning track in right field, but he caught the ball. And I had the first no-hitter of my career.

My teammates mobbed me and were jumping up and down and screaming. Jeff Torborg was really excited. "Oh, God, Nolan," he kept saying. "That was beautiful, that was beautiful."

I honestly never felt I was the type of pitcher to throw a no-hitter. I was happy to have it, but I didn't show much emotion. I never allow myself to get too high in good times or too low in the bad times. That way I feel I can keep things in perspective.

It was a getaway game, and we had to rush to get out of there. I did manage to call Ruth, and she was thrilled.

"That was great, Nolan, just great!" she said.

"I guess it was okay," I said. "I'm just happy that it's over."

The next day there was a lot in the newspapers about the no-hitter. Hal McRae of the Royals gave me some nice praise. "If they had a higher league than the majors," McRae said, "Ryan would be in it . . . as a matter of fact he could be it."

That first no-hitter gave me a good deal of publicity, that and my wildness and my strikeouts. National magazines did stories about me, and I got much more press attention than ever before. I was the same person I always was, but a kind of mythology about me started to develop. Part of it came from what others said about me.

BROOKS ROBINSON:

Is there fear of Ryan? Sure there's fear. There's an old baseball saying: "Your heart might be in the batter's box, but your ass ain't."

DAVE DUNCAN:

You had to respect pitchers like Catfish Hunter. He had that perfect control. But a guy like Ryan doesn't just get you out. He embarrasses you. There are times when you've won some sort of victory just hitting the ball.

HERB SCORE:

He's spectacular. What people don't realize is that he has a great curve. All the great fastball pitchers did. . . . With someone like Ryan there is always the possibility of a strikeout record or a no-hitter.

On July 3, 1973, Sal Bando of Oakland became my 1,000th career strikeout. Twelve days later—exactly two months to the date that I pitched my first no-hitter—I got my second.

Warming up before the game in Detroit on July 15, 1973, I knew I had good stuff. I had a hard curve and good velocity. When I came out onto the field from the bullpen, I told Tom Morgan, "With the kind of stuff I have now, if I ever have a chance to pitch another no-hitter it'll be today."

I made a decision to call every one of my own pitches in that game because we thought the Tigers were trying to pick up our signs. My catcher, Art Kusnyer, would just give any old signal, and I would make believe I was taking it, but I was actually ignoring it.

The deal we set up went this way: if I touched the back of my cap, that meant that I was going to throw a fastball; if I touched the front of my cap, I would throw a curve. Art relayed the pitch I was going to throw to the infielders.

I threw a hard curve that broke down for the first pitch of the game. But Art and I had gotten the signs mixed up. Art was looking for the fastball and never laid his glove on the ball. It went right by him on the fly and hit Ron Luciano, the home plate umpire that game, square on the knee.

RON LUCIANO:

That first pitch Ryan threw was a sharp curve that broke down as if it had fallen off the edge of a cliff and bounced off catcher Art Kusnyer's shin guard. Uh oh, I thought, if that was his curveball, we're in trouble today. Kusnyer turned around to me. "My God, Nolan's going to throw a no-hitter. Anybody who can throw that hard on the first pitch—one that I couldn't even see, let alone catch it—has got to pitch a no-hitter."

My first pitch was called a ball. "Ron," I yelled, "how could that pitch have been a ball if it hit you right on the knee and it came square over the middle of the plate and you were standing behind the catcher?"

Luciano didn't answer. I thought if that was the way it was going to be, I was in for a long day. Although my curveballs were breaking more than a foot, I didn't bother throwing many in the game. My fastball had so much pop that I just made up my mind to go with it.

RON LUCIANO:

From the first pitch Nolan threw, there was no question the batters would have no chance. That game when he wanted to hit an inside corner—he hit an inside corner. When he wanted to throw letter-high—he threw letter-high. It was the most perfect pitching I've ever seen in my life.

The feeling of power, of being in complete control, made me feel like the king of the hill, made me feel pretty early in the game that I had a shot at the no-hitter.

Billy Martin, the Tiger manager then, probably sensed it, too. Not the most refined kind of guy, Billy yelled all kinds of stuff at me, trying to break my concentration. I remember Billy shouting, "[Aurelio] Rodriguez is gonna homer off you now! You lose the no-hitter on the next pitch."

I stared at Martin in the dugout. "No way, Billy," I hollered. And then I struck out Rodriguez. I looked back into the Tiger dugout, but Billy turned his back and wouldn't face me. That gave me a charge.

The fans in Detroit made a racket, and so did some of the Tiger players. None of that bothered me. I just zoned in on what I had to do.

RON LUCIANO:

Ryan's ball left the pitcher's mound as big as a golf ball and when it reached the plate it exploded into a million blinding white specks. Some of the hitters would just look at me like they couldn't believe it or when he threw that curve say, "Jeezuz!"

I called three straight strikes on Mickey Stanley: "Boom! Sounds low on the corner. Boom! Sounds like the inside corner of the plate. Boom! Sounds like you're out."

Stanley turned around and said, "Thank you."

I said, "What?"

"I couldn't hit one of those pitches no matter what," Stanley said. "Those were the greatest pitches I ever heard."

I struck out sixteen batters through the first seven innings, but the game was a close one. We had only a 1–0 lead. Then in the top of the eighth my teammates batted around and scored five runs to break open the game.

Waiting around all that time while the scoring was going on, I could feel I was getting stiff. I was anxious to get going because I'm not like some pitchers who can use the extra rest. I knew with the layoff I was going to lose some movement on the ball. Pitching in the bottom of the eighth inning, I knew I didn't have the same stuff. They were hitting my pitches. There was less pop in my fastball. I managed to pick up just one more strikeout in the last two innings, making it seventeen for the game—the most any pitcher ever had in a no-hitter.

I worked carefully to Mickey Stanley, the first Tiger batter in the ninth inning, and got him on a grounder. Left-handed-hitting Gates Brown came up. He was one of the premier designated hitters in the American League at that time, a good low-fastball hitter. I got behind in the count and felt I had to throw him a fastball. Gates hit a hard line drive to the left side of the infield. I was worried when the ball hit the bat, thinking it was going to go through the infield. But it was hit right at Rudy Meoli, our shortstop. If Gates had hit that ball a foot or two either way it would have been a base hit, maybe even a double to the wall. It shows how quite a bit of luck goes into the pitching of a no-hitter.

With one out left to Detroit, Norm Cash came up. I had struck Norm out twice. He was the only thing standing between me and the no-hitter—unless you include Ron Luciano. A lot of people disliked Ron because he was so colorful and had so much showmanship. Some of the other umpires were even a bit jealous of him because of all the attention he got. I always thought Ron was a dynamic guy and a fine umpire. When Ron umpired behind the plate, he gave me a good effort, although there were times when he could get distracted.

I looked at Norm stepping into the batter's box, and I knew what he was holding in his hands wasn't a baseball bat.

"Ron, what's he got?"

Luciano acted as if I was bothering him. "What're you talking about?"

"Check his bat!" I shouted. "Check that thing."

Luciano took the piece of wood out of Norm's hand and looked it over. I found out later it was a leg he had ripped off the snack table in the clubhouse.

"Norm, you can't bat with this old piano leg." Ron was scolding Norm like a child. "Get rid of it."

"But, Ron, I've got no chance with a bat. Lemme try this."

"Get rid of it!"

"But, Ron, that Ryan hit me on the arm one time, and it was the hardest I ever got hit. It even busted the seam on the ball. I ain't gonna hit him anyway. Lemme use this thing."

"Get rid of it."

Norm got rid of it, and that incident helped get rid of some of the tension I was feeling. Everyone had his laugh, including me.

Then I went to work on Norm—throwing nothing but fastballs. On a 1–2 count, he hit a little pop-up to short left. Meoli caught it, and I became only the fifth pitcher in history to get two no-hitters in one season.

Art Kusnyer, who'd caught the first no-hitter of his career, was going around showing off his bruised fingers and banged-up palm and talking about how any kind of padding was totally useless with the kind of heat I was throwing.

I heard later that a bunch of kids came over to Detroit's catcher, Duke Sims, after the game and asked for a cracked bat. "Weren't you watching the game?" Sims said, laughing. "We didn't hit the ball hard enough to crack any bats. But maybe Norm Cash can sell you a table leg cheap. It wasn't even used."

Another time we were playing Detroit, and before the

game I told Jeff Torborg, who was catching, that I thought we needed to pitch Norm in because I felt he was looking for the ball out over the plate. The first time up, we started Norm off with a fastball in. The ball hit him on the elbow and Norm went down like he'd been shot. I thought I had broken his arm. After a couple of minutes, instead of walking off the field, Norm crawled to the dugout.

I saw him after the game and went over to check out his condition. "How's your arm, Norm? I hope nothing is broken."

Norm gave me a big, wide smile. "Kid, don't worry about a thing. After four pain-killers and a fifth of Jack Daniel's I'm feeling just fine."

Another time we were playing in Detroit and I was pitching to Norm, and he surprised me by managing to get a hold of one of my pitches. He lofted a lazy fly ball deep to right field. There was a runner on third base, so I backed up behind home plate because I thought he might tag up and we'd have a play at the plate. He didn't tag, so there wasn't a throw. Before I walked back to the mound I took a look at Norm's bat lying there near home plate. At the end of the bat there was a big round circle. I knew right away what that circle meant: Norm's bat was corked. I figured I'd save that information for a more dramatic moment.

The next time Norm came up to face me in the game I told the umpire, "Check his bat."

"What?" the umpire asked.

"Check his bat," I told him. "You'll see that he's corked the end of it."

Norm put on the most innocent look a guy like him was capable of while the umpire inspected his bat. Seeing that the bat was plugged, the umpire removed it from play. But I'm sure the next game Norm was back again hitting with the same bat.

Strange situations were commonplace for Norm. He was a true character. One time he chased after a foul ball that was hit outside the first base line. When he got near the stands and realized he had no chance to catch the foul ball he settled for something else. He stood at the edge of the stands, reached out, and took a free handful out of a fan's cup of popcorn.

One time I was on first base at Anaheim Stadium after having gotten a base hit. Norm congratulated me in his peculiar style. "Nice going, kid," he said. "I didn't know you had it in you." I started to take my lead off the base. Norm moved closer to me and began talking about Texas and dogs and cattle and hunting. He sure knew the topics that interested me. He had a real gift of the gab, and I got so interested in our conversation that I was more involved in talking to him that paying attention to the Tiger pitcher. The next thing I knew, the pitcher had picked me off first base. That aggravated me no end. That old veteran Norm Cash sure showed me one of the tricks of his trade and taught me a lesson at the same time.

Norm Cash passed away in October of 1986, and I felt sad about that. He was a free spirit, a good man, one of the true characters of the game.

I got a lot of attention from the media after pitching my

first no-hitter, but after the second there was more than ever. And all of that was tough on a guy like me who always liked to be a private person.

Some reporters ask the same question until they get the answer they have in mind. One guy went into the old story about Johnny Vander Meer pitching those back-to-back no-hitters for the Cincinnati Reds June of 1938.

"Nolan," the guy asked, "do you think you can pitch another no-hitter in your next start and tie Vander Meer's record?"

"I don't think so," I told him. "I honestly think it will be easier for me to strike out twenty than pitch another no-hitter."

That answer was no good for him. "But, Nolan, you've got such overpowering stuff—it could be possible, couldn't it?"

"Possible," I said, "but hardly probable."

"But it could happen?" That reporter was real pushy.

"I guess," I said; "I guess it could." And he finally let me alone.

The game after that second no-hitter was against Baltimore, a tough ball club. I was uncomfortable about that start. With all the media hype, I felt very distracted. Considering it was Anaheim, a large crowd showed up anticipating another no-hitter. And I went out there with that intent—to throw another no-hitter. It was the first time and the last time I ever approached a game like that. Going for a no-hitter puts added pressure on you, makes you work harder than you usually do, because each pitch has the potential to end or extend the no-hitter. In that game each hitter I faced wore me out as I concentrated on getting that no-hitter. I had very good velocity, but I was also very wild.

Throughout the game Baltimore's manager, Earl Weaver, kept getting on me. He made the umps look at the ball a few times, claiming that I was using pine tar or Vaseline. I have never used anything like that.

That was just Weaver's way of trying to irritate me. Managers like Weaver, Billy Martin, and Chuck Tanner were always very antagonistic to me when I pitched. I think they felt that because I threw hard and was wild they could rattle me. I've never let anything any bench jockey said bother me. I just concentrate on doing my job.

I have tunnel vision. It was something I didn't always have. It took several years to develop the ability to block out everything that goes on at the ballpark, to concentrate totally on what I am doing on the mound. Some days this is easier said than done.

There's a zone, a tunnel, that goes from me in a straight line to my catcher. I know the hitter is there, but I hardly notice him at all. I am throwing to my catcher, who I have set up on the corners of the plate. If I paid attention to what the hitter is doing, it would break my concentration. I just zone in on my catcher.

In that game against Baltimore after my second no-hitter, going into the eighth inning I was zoned in. I still had a no-hitter going, but the score was 1–1. The Orioles had scored on a walk, a stolen base, a wild pitch, and a ground ball. I was worn down from throwing so many pitches.

Brooks Robinson led off the eighth inning for Baltimore, and I hit him with a pitch. That brought up Mark Belanger, who was hitting just a bit over .200. Mark choked up a lot on the bat and could always hit fastball pitchers. He didn't hit them hard, but he could get the bat on the ball and hit a lot of flares, using the entire field. He usually hit me to right, so now we shifted him that way.

Belanger was up there bunting and missed the first pitch. I figured he'd try to bunt again, so my second pitch to him was high and inside. He swung and the pitch jammed him, and he just blooped the ball out to left center field.

Ken Berry came charging in from right center, but the ball managed to fall in for a base hit. It was just one of those balls hit in the right place, which is an example of why no-hitters are so hard to throw. Later Belanger said, "If Ken Berry had been playing me straightaway in the outfield, he would have caught the ball easily."

When I lost the no-hitter and came within six outs of tying Johnny Vander Meer's record, I was disappointed that I'd gotten that close with no success. But I was relieved that the whole thing was over with. I wound up not only losing the no-hitter but also losing the game in the eleventh inning, 3–1. The effort had been physically and emotionally exhausting.

In 1973 I struck out ten or more batters in a game twenty-three times to break another major league record set by Sandy Koufax. He had twenty-one games where he struck out ten or more in 1965. One of those games was the one I saw him pitch at the Dome when I was a high school kid. That 1973 season I struck out eight in a row against Milwaukee to duplicate what I had done against Boston the year before.

That season has to rank as the high-water mark of my career. Not only did I pitch two no-hitters, but as the season drew toward its end I became only the third pitcher in history along with Sandy Koufax and Rube Waddell to strike out 300 batters two years in a row.

The all-time season strikeout record belonged to Sandy —382 strikeouts. Once I passed 300 strikeouts all the hype and hoopla started about my breaking that record. I was interested in breaking the record but really didn't know if I had a good shot at it. I had thrown and would throw in the seasons to come a lot of pitches. With the Angels, I averaged nearly 300 innings and more than 35 starts a season.

JEFF TORBORG:

Nolan would throw a tremendous amount of pitches in a game —150 to 200—and they would all be awesome. He threw so hard that he would occasionally choke the ball. And the bottom of the ball would fall out like a sinkerball. But Nolan is not a sinkerballer—he's a blazer.

Once in a game in Detroit we got crossed up on a pitch. I was looking curve and it was a fastball. It missed the glove and hit the back of my hand. I had to go get X rays. I had a real bad bruise, but fortunately my hand was not broken. Nolan's comment was "I must be losing my fastball."

In 1973 I started using a new glove. The pounding his fastball gave that glove made it tear a little bit as the season went on. I kept taking it to a shoemaker and he kept patching it up. By the end of the season the glove had a big white patch on it. "I like that," Nolan told me. "It's like a target in there for me to shoot at."

That glove took a heck of a beating. Once in a game in Boston he threw one of his fastballs right through the webbing of the glove. It tore right through it on the fly and hit the backstop. It was kind of a frightening sensation. I wondered what might have happened if that ball had been thrown down in front of me. Oh, man!

It was nice to read a comment by Whitey Herzog, then the Texas manager, that "Nolan Ryan has the greatest arm in the history of baseball." But as my strikeouts increased— I would wind up striking out ten or more batters in a game twenty-three times in '73, a new major league record—as I got closer to the Koufax record, so did the pressure and the fatigue.

Through it all, though, I was pitching pretty well, winning consistently for a change, getting some breaks. That season I won eight of my last ten decisions. And I won my twentieth victory in a wild game against Minnesota.

It was a struggle—I gave up eleven hits in the final four innings—but we outlasted the Twins 15–7. I was thankful that my teammates gave me a lot of runs to work with. This wasn't an artistic game, but it still was a big win.

Going into the final week of the season I was sixteen strikeouts shy of the Sandy Koufax record. My last scheduled start, my thirty-ninth of the year, was against Minnesota at Anaheim on a Thursday night.

"Good luck," Ruth said, as I left the house to go to the park. She would arrive around game time.

"Thanks, I'll need all the luck I can get," I told her.

"Don't take any chances out there," Ruth said. "You have your whole career ahead of you, and the strikeout record isn't worth risking your arm. You'll have other chances."

"We'll see what happens, Ruth. You know, if I don't get the sixteen tonight, I can still come back on Sunday in our final game of the year and try to get whatever I need for the record."

I had trouble right off the bat in the first inning. The Twins hit two singles and a double and scored three runs. I didn't even have a strikeout. It almost looked as if I wasn't going to make it through the first.

Bobby Winkles, who had taken over in 1973, replacing Del Rice as manager, came out to the mound. He was concerned.

"Are you all right, Nolan?"

"I think so," I said. "I just haven't gotten loose yet."

"All right, then. Get loose. You've got a lot of pitching to do."

Jim Holt was the next hitter and my first strikeout. After the first inning, I seemed to find my rhythm. Only fifteen more strikeouts, I thought. This could be a long day.

In the bottom of the first, my usually weak-hitting teammates came up with three runs and tied the score. That relieved some of the pressure on me. It's always much easier to pitch when you're ahead, or at least tied.

Through the first five innings I struck out a dozen batters. Then I struck out the side in the seventh. All I needed was one more strikeout, and I would have the record.

Looking back on that game, it was one of the funniest of all my baseball experiences in a strange sort of way: the roar of the crowd between each pitch, the quiet when the ball was on its way to the batter, the groan from all those people when a batter popped up or grounded out. Those Angel fans wanted the out, but they wanted the out to be made on a strikeout.

The game moved into the bottom of the ninth. The score was still 3–3. And I still needed one more strikeout for the record. We had a chance to win the game in the bottom of the ninth but couldn't do it. The crowd was relieved, however, that we couldn't, that the game was going into extra innings. It was the only time in my career that I was witness to a home crowd rooting against its own team.

The game moved through the tenth inning and into the eleventh. Bobby Winkles was concerned about my physical condition.

"Nolan, this is your last inning," he said. "No matter what, you can't go on—you're flat out exhausted."

I was exhausted, and I knew that I'd never be able to come back on Sunday. The eleventh inning would be it. I'd get the record or I wouldn't get the record.

I got two strikes on Steve Brye. The crowd was really into it now. They came up roaring when he went around on my next pitch and it seemed for an instant that I had the strikeout, but it was a foul tip. On the next pitch Brye popped out. I was still looking for the record, and those Minnesota batters were still looking not to go into the record book with me.

I walked Rod Carew, and Bobby Winkles came out to visit with me on the mound. The crowd booed, thinking he was going to take me out.

"How do you feel, Nolan?" he asked.

"Okay," I said. "I'll get through with it."

Winkles walked back to the Angel dugout, leaving me in, and the crowd gave him a big ovation.

I got a strike on Tony Oliva and then he was out on a fly ball. The crowd groaned again. Rich Reese came up to hit. With one out left to them, he was my last chance to break the record. I knew I couldn't go on past that inning, and I was certain that I could not come back on Sunday.

I walked off the mound, took a few deep breaths, and decided I was going to throw as hard as I could.

Reese swung and missed. The crowd was standing on its feet and roaring. Reese swung and missed again. Carew took off for second base.

JEFF TORBORG:

I threw a perfect strike down to second base. When I let that throw go I thought to myself, Why now? Why my best throw of the season now? Carew was called safe on a very close play. The crowd cheered, and then it started to boo me.

I wasn't distracted. I looked in at Jeff for my target and threw the ball as hard as I could. Reese swung from his heels—and came up empty. The all-time single-season strikeout record—383—was mine.

My teammates surged from the dugout to offer their congratulations and led me back to the bench. The fans were on their feet for about four minutes applauding, cheering. I came out of the dugout and tipped my cap to them. I was spent in every way, yet on an emotional high, something rare for me.

The quest for strikeout number 383 seemed to have taken forever. And now that it was over, I savored the moment. That was one of the highlights of my baseball career—breaking one of the records of Sandy Koufax, a player I had always looked up to.

Besides the single-season strikeout record, in 1973 I had 21 wins for a mediocre fourth-place team that won just 79 games, tied Milwaukee for the lowest batting average, and was next to last in runs scored in the American League. I was fourth among all American League pitchers in earned run average and second in complete games. I also pitched the two no-hitters. There were those who thought I should have had at least one more credited to me.

JEFF TORBORG:

In a game against the New York Yankees, Thurman Munson hit a pop-up behind second base. Rudi Meoli and Sandy Alomar kind of came together and the ball fell in. The official scorer called it a base hit. That was in the first inning. If it had been later in the game they might have done something about it. If a catcher misses a pop-up they'll give him an error—why not out on the field? That was the only "hit" Nolan gave up.

I caught both Koufax and Ryan and there were lots of similarities between them and some differences. Both threw over the top. Sandy had the best curveball I'd ever seen. It was straight down and awesome. Nolan had a smaller curve, with not as big a rotation as Sandy's but with very similar action.

Nolan threw the ball harder down in the strike zone than anyone I've ever seen. That was a thing we really worked on. I kept harping on him to throw down to the outer half of the plate, the outer corner.

Sandy and Nolan are outstanding athletes, and they could have done anything they wanted to in sports. They're both very quiet men, private personalities. Both of them are very tough. The great ability was always there with Sandy and Nolan, but even more—they wanted it. They wanted it a little more than the rest of us. They were at a level where they belonged in another league. I'll always remember catching them—they were the kind of pitchers who made a mediocre catcher look pretty good.

RON LUCIANO:

I was umpiring behind the plate in one game. Ryan was pitching, and things were going along all right. Then in the fifth inning, this pitch of Ryan's came up to the plate. I couldn't believe my eyes. There was no cover on the ball. Oh my God, I thought, he threw the cover off the ball.

I didn't yell "Ball" or "Strike." I just ducked down behind the catcher. I didn't want to get hit. When I came back up, the catcher was throwing the ball out to Ryan on the mound. But now the cover was back on the ball. Oh oh, I thought, I've got trouble with my eyes.

The next day I went to see an ophthalmologist. He was a highly regarded doctor who also happened to know a lot about baseball. I explained to him that, the night before, I saw Nolan Ryan throw a pitch so hard I thought the cover came off the ball.

"So what's the problem?" the ophthalmologist asked.

"You don't understand," I screamed at him. "I'm an umpire, and I saw something that didn't happen."

"Settle down, Ron," the doctor said kindly. "Let me explain. With most pitchers the ball leaves their hands the size of a golf ball and appears bigger and bigger as it comes to the plate."

"What's all this got to do with my vision?" I said, getting more and more impatient.

"I'm getting to that. Ryan might have thrown the ball you saw at 100.9, 102, 103 miles an hour. At that speed, when it came up to the plate, it looked like it blew up. It looked like the cover came off the ball."

"So?" I still didn't get it.

"So," the doc continued, "what you saw was an optical illusion, something that didn't really happen. But you don't have to worry about it, Ron. Nolan Ryan's the only pitcher who can throw that hard."

"You sure, Doc?"

"I'm sure. Those balls are not your problem. They're the hitters' problem."

Boy, was I relieved. I had used the words "exploding fastball" before in my life, but I never knew what the words meant. That night with Nolan I saw an "exploding fastball." It was the only time I ever saw one. It still is spellbinding to think about. . . .

A lot was written about me being the leading candidate for the Cy Young Award for 1973, and some of the writers were saying that I was the best pitcher in baseball. All of that kind of publicity has to have an effect on a person, and maybe I got to believing it was all true. To tell the truth, I was sort of expecting to win the Cy Young Award, but things don't always turn out the way you expect them to.

I was back in Alvin after the season ended, working on my ranch with my dogs in a back pasture, when a sportswriter called Ruth and gave her the news. It wasn't until it got dark and I returned to the house that I found out that Jim Palmer had won the Cy Young Award and that I'd finished second.

"That's the way it goes," I told Ruth. "I wanted that award, but I didn't get it. And I'm not going to worry about it or let it affect my attitude or my pitching."

It was a disappointment finishing second to Palmer, but he'd been a big winner for years and never won the award, so I guess it was his time. What irritated me, though, was what he said about me. Jim Palmer has never been a big fan of mine, and why that is I don't know. But instead of being gracious in accepting the award he decided to attack me, saying that he deserved it more than me. He said that I went for strikeouts and that he went for outs. I always thought that strikeouts and outs were the same thing, and I meant to ask Jim Palmer what he meant by that comment. But I never got to speak to him about it. I considered Jim Palmer to be a prima donna, always complaining about his team not scoring runs for him. In my opinion he was a player who was always out for himself and not really too concerned about his team.

Although I didn't get the Cy Young Award, the Angels rewarded me for what I had accomplished in 1973 by giving me a salary raise to $100,000 a year. That was a lot of money back then. They also had a night in my honor, and considering I had just finished my second season with the team, that was something special. Other players on their nights get fancy cars. I wound up with a pickup truck. I think they thought I could find a use for it.

Although the Angels were a struggling team, I was comfortable being there with them. Gene Autry was the best owner I have ever played for. He was a real fan. "With baseball," he said, "I sleep like a baby. I wake up and cry for a while, go back to sleep, wake up, and cry a little more."

When I was a boy living in Alvin I went with my family to the Houston Livestock Show and Rodeo. My youngest sister and I went down to the rail of the arena where Gene Autry, the entertainer that night, was signing autographs and shaking hands. I never collected autographs, but I did shake Gene's hand. That was the first time I had ever seen

Gene Autry. It's funny how things happen; who would ever have thought I would end up pitching for him?

If you didn't know who he was, you'd say Gene Autry was just a wealthy guy who lived in Palm Springs. He'd come down to the clubhouse prior to games and sit around and talk to the players in casual conversation. Gene was like the good guy in the white hat. We got to be pretty friendly with each other. He knew I was a diehard Texan, and we'd spend a lot of time talking about Texas.

RON LUCIANO:

I always thought all the Texas cowboys were tall fellas like Nolan—six foot, twenty. Then I met Gene Autry. I had to look down to make eye contact with him. I know why Gene Autry liked Nolan so much. Nolan was exactly what Gene had always wanted to be: a great pitcher and a tall Texan.

Gene was a fun-loving guy, a man who enjoyed having a good time. Once at a "Welcome Back, Angels," dinner in Palm Springs hosted by the Chamber of Commerce, Gene had a few extra drinks during the cocktail hour. Before the dinner began, he got up to deliver a speech. Looking over the crowd, he said, "I've never seen so many beautiful women, all dressed up, like there are here tonight. You all remind me of a flower garden . . . so many beautiful flowers." He looked around the room, then added, "But in any flower garden, there are always some weeds. Don't look around; you know who you are." That was Gene. He had his own sense of humor.

I was at one black-tie dinner, and Gene Autry was there, all dressed up in his tuxedo. Then I looked down, and I saw he was wearing black cowboy boots. And I thought, if there's anyone in the world who could wear cowboy boots on an occasion like that, it's Gene Autry.

Gene was good friends with Richard Nixon, who was an American League fan from his days in Washington, when he followed the Senators. Anaheim Stadium was reasonably close to Nixon's home in San Clemente, so he would come to our games and sit up in Gene Autry's private box. On occasion Nixon would come down to the clubhouse and visit and talk baseball.

One time after I'd pitched the first game of a doubleheader at Anaheim Stadium, Gene Autry telephoned down to the clubhouse. "Say, Nolan," he said, "how about coming up to my box to watch the second game? Richard Nixon is up here with me."

So I went up and we sat there and watched the game and just visited. When the seventh-inning stretch time came around, Richard Nixon stood up. "Let's wave to the fans," he said to me, so I waved to the fans along with him.

A picture was taken of us waving, and they ran it in the Los Angeles *Times* the next day. That picture started one guy off. I began to receive hate letters from this guy telling me I shouldn't associate with a traitor and Communist like Richard Nixon.

I was getting those letters for about three or four weeks. Finally I sent the guy a photograph of myself and I autographed it to him: "To a great Angel fan, always look forward to hearing from you." That did the trick. I never heard another word from the guy.

Nixon was about the only regular celebrity we had at Anaheim. We never had celebrities the way the Dodgers did because we were about thirty miles from downtown Los Angeles, on the wrong side of L.A. for the Hollywood set. We always felt like the stepchild to Los Angeles because we didn't have a major media center in Anaheim. All the correspondents had to come down from L.A. to cover our games—and it was a long trip, since most of the time the Angels weren't doing anything that excited them too much.

In June of 1974 Dick Williams came in as manager, replacing Whitey Herzog, who had been a temporary replacement for Bobby Winkles. Bobby had made a big name for himself as the baseball coach at Arizona State and was a really nice guy, but maybe too nice to manage in the majors. I think some previous professional managing would have been good for him.

When Dick Williams—who no one ever accused of being too nice—came in, Tom Morgan left. I don't know if it was because Dick wanted his own people or because Tom thought it was just time to move on.

In six seasons as a manager Dick Williams had won two world championships, three American League pennants, and three divisional titles. He was used to winning, but the Angels weren't.

Even with their differences and their feuding, that Oakland team that Dick managed always played well. The

Angels were a different story. We were in a building process. We had some players who were in the majors only
because they were being force-fed. Today Dick is probably
much better equipped to handle a situation like that, but
back then he put a lot of pressure on the young kids and he
had trouble coping with the inabilities of his players. One
on one, though, I got along very well with Dick and had no
problems with him. He was always fair and honest with me.
I liked him as a person. When he was working as a manager, however, he became very aggressive. Dick knows his
baseball and has a lot of knowledge of tactics. With the
Angels he was the kind of manager who got a lot out of a
team and required a lot of things from his players. But after
a while, with the way he bore down, he wore thin, and a lot
of players resented him for his tough approach.

Gene Autry had paid Oakland owner Charles Finley
$50,000 for the right to sign Williams as manager of the
Angels, and Gene thought he'd gotten a miracle worker.
But Dick lost the first ten games he managed, and Gene
was fit to be tied. He came into the clubhouse and he was
steaming.

Whitey Herzog's record was 2–2 as an interim manager
after Winkles left. Gene spotted Whitey and then looked at
Williams and yelled, "God damn, I think I hired the wrong
manager."

Both Whitey and Dick are excellent managers, but the
Angels at that time just didn't have the talent. We had a
bunch of young and inexperienced players and some others who were veterans, just playing out their careers. It

made for a situation where I went out there each time trying to shut out everybody. It seemed we were always mathematically eliminated by August. Our teams had some trouble catching the ball. They couldn't hit too much either, and that made for a lot of jokes.

Once our catcher Tom Egan was hit by a line drive during batting practice. "Thank God it was one of our guys who hit the ball," Dick Williams said, "or else Tom would've been hurt bad."

Bill Lee, a pitcher for Boston, was quoted as saying to Dick, "Your team has such a bunch of weak hitters that you can get them to take batting practice in a hotel lobby and they won't break anything." Dick followed Bill's suggestion and staged a little batting drill in the Sheraton-Boston Hotel. Bill was right. Nothing was broken.

And then there was Bill Melton, the third baseman for the Chicago White Sox, who bobbled a few balls hit at him by Angel batters. "Don't get on me for my fielding," he told reporters later. "Those Angels never hit the ball hard enough for it to be fielded cleanly."

That 1974 season George Lederer, the public relations director for the Angels, came up with a special promotion contest involving me. Fans were asked to send in postcards on which they'd write down what they thought my top velocity would be in a game. The rules of the contest promised a free trip to Hawaii to the person who came closest to picking my highest speed.

I didn't like the hype and the carnival-type atmosphere. I felt that it distracted from what I was trying to do as a pitcher: concentrate on winning ball games, not setting speed records. But it reflected the Angels' situation, so I agreed to go along with it. We didn't have a very good ball club and we were trying to do something to put fans in the stands and build more interest in the team.

The whole thing was very scientific. Rockwell International scientists came in with all kinds of sophisticated electronic equipment. Using the game before the actual test game as an experiment, they timed my pitching and gave no results. But it was done that way to iron out all the bugs that might've come up.

The way the deal worked is that technicians shot a beam from the press box down in front of home plate. But the beam covered only about 30 percent of the strike zone—the middle of home plate—so it didn't really pick up all of my pitches. Also, you don't really ever pitch to the middle of the plate.

The game I was timed in for the record was on August 20, 1974, against the Chicago White Sox. The Rockwell people's plan was to record my last five warm-up pitches and put the results on the board to show the fans how it worked.

I went out and warmed up in the bullpen and then came onto the mound and threw my warm-up pitches. The first pitch I threw was clocked at 74 miles an hour, and they put that result on the board. I remember looking out there and thinking to myself, Well, this is going to be embarrassing, because the record had always been 98.6 by Bob Feller. He was timed at that speed in 1946 by the Army, using something they called lumiline chronography. My next pitch was about 79 miles per hour, then I went up to 83, and I ended up getting to 92. One of my pitches didn't record because it didn't go through the beam they were shooting down.

I set the record in the ninth inning against Bee Bee Richard. It was a 3–2 high fastball at 100.9 mph. And at that speed, they said the ball crossed home plate in 0.38 seconds.

I don't know if that was the fastest pitch I threw in that game, and I know I have thrown faster pitches in my career, but that pitch stands as the all-time record—100.9 mph.

In that particular game I didn't feel like I had my best stuff even though seven of my pitches were clocked at more than 100 miles an hour. I threw about 150 pitches in the game and don't recall how many pitches they recorded, but they certainly missed some of them. They didn't flash the speed of that 100.9 mph pitch on the board; they announced it after the game.

When that record was set that night I didn't think anything about it because I felt that was not my best velocity ever. But Bob Feller was quoted: "I'm not quibbling, mind you, but comparing the way we were timed is like comparing apples and oranges." Bob Feller has always been a big critic of mine. I think he has a little trouble with the changes of time.

To this day you get people that will argue about fastball pitchers in different eras, and you'll never have people agree on who was the fastest. You hear stories that they got

J. R. Richard at 100, Lee Smith at 99, and Goose Gossage at 99.4.

But those speeds are on radar guns, and every one of those guns varies. You can line four guns up there and throw one pitch, and you may get four different readings. On the radar gun in Houston, for example, where they record every pitch thrown in the Dome, only one time have they ever recorded a pitch at 100 miles an hour. And that was a pitch I threw in 1985.

Now they use a different gun, a slower gun, in Houston. But once you get over 90 miles an hour there's as much as a 2–3 mph variance in those guns. You can't really put much stock in those figures. My timing in that game in August of 1974 was done by scientists using sophisticated equipment, and that's why the *Guinness Book of World Records* recognizes that as the record for the fastest pitch ever thrown.

One of the most frightening moments in my career took place in 1974. That was also related to the speed and movement of my pitches. I was pitching to Boston's second baseman Doug Griffin, who was up there to bunt. Knowing this, I tried to get the ball up so he'd pop it up.

But the ball rode in on Griffin. He froze and the ball hit him behind his left ear. He fell to the ground. I didn't think anything about it until I walked up to the plate and saw him lying unconscious on the ground. At first I thought he was dead. I got a sick feeling realizing that one of my pitches could kill somebody.

After the game I obtained Griffin's home phone number. I wanted to speak to his wife to tell her I was sorry about what had happened and ask her if there was anything I could do. "My mommy is not home," said the little girl who answered the phone. "She went to the hospital to be with my daddy."

That incident and talking to Doug's daughter bothered me a lot. Doug's daughter seemed to be about the same age as my son Reid. I wondered what it would be like if someone called and spoke to Reid when I was lying in the hospital after having been hit by a fastball. If you're a sensitive person—and I'm a sensitive person even though I may not appear that way on the mound—things like that have to bother you. I knew the Sandy Koufax line: "Show me a guy who can't pitch inside and I'll show you a loser." But what had happened with Griffin bothered me so much that I quit throwing pitches inside for a time.

After missing fifty-one games, Griffin came back from the beaning. His first game was against me, and I was a little sensitive about facing him. I pitched him nothing but away his first two times up, and he leaned in and got two ground-ball hits. I realized then that I had to block out what had happened from my mind. I had no choice but to block it out or I'd become a defensive pitcher instead of an aggressive one. The next time Griffin came up I pitched him inside, and I got him out. Pitching inside is part of the game. Baseball is a business and you have to do what's necessary to win.

Some hitters show more fear than others, and when you know that, you pitch accordingly. The inside fastball is part of the game. When you throw inside, all those other hitters sitting on the bench see that. As a pitcher you need any kind of mental edge you can get, any kind of distraction. Hitters won't be looking for a pitch away if they know I'm coming inside. Although a lot of first base and third base coaches will pick up the pitches—or a pitcher will tip off his pitches and a sign will be sent to the batter of what's coming—some hitters will not take the sign. That's because they don't want to be looking for a curveball over the plate and get a fastball inside that they can't get away from.

ALAN ASHBY:

> The funniest line I ever heard about Nolan was said by Oscar Gamble. We were teammates on Cleveland and were driving up to Anaheim Stadium. The marquee advertised: "Nolan Ryan versus the Cleveland Indians." Oscar turned to me and said, "A good night tonight is 0 for 4 and don't get hit in the head."

Despite the fact that some batters through the years have been gun-shy about hitting against me, I've never tried to hit a batter—except for one time in a game against Boston at Anaheim. In that game I was walking a lot of people and striking out a lot of people. The players on the Boston bench were screaming at me, "Throw harder. Throw harder!"

I became angry and frustrated. I looked over at the Boston bench, and a couple of guys were standing there on the top step of the dugout. They were yelling at me. One of them, I thought, was Rick Miller.

That's fine, I decided. Rick's in the lineup and he's got to hit again. The next time Rick came up I tried to hit him. I threw three pitches and knocked him down each time, but kept missing him. I finally got him with my fourth pitch— right square in the ribs. Then I walked up to home plate while he was lying on the ground to see if he had anything else to say. He didn't. He just got up and rubbed a little bit and went down to first base. That was the end of that.

Over the winter Boston traded him to us. In spring training Rick and I got to talking. "Why'd you hit me in the ribs last year?" he asked.

"You had an awful lot to say about me."

"I didn't say anything, Nolan. It wasn't me doing all the yelling."

"Well then," I told Rick, "I'm truly sorry. I guess it was just a case of mistaken identity."

I had never thrown to hit anyone before that time and I never threw to hit anyone again. There weren't many opportunities, anyway. Even when I went through periods when I was very wild and some teams would get on me, most of the players wouldn't get involved. They knew they would have to hit off me and they didn't want to be singled out as a possible target.

I've seen a lot of baseball played in my more than two decades in the major leagues. Some of it I've only witnessed and some of it I've participated in. There have been seven 19-strikeout games pitched in the modern era—and I've in one way or another been a part of most of them.

On June 14, 1974, in a game against the Boston Red Sox, I

struck out 19 batters in 12 innings and threw 235 pitches. That was 6 shy of my all-time record for pitches thrown in a game.

Then on August 12 I faced the Red Sox again and struck out 19 in 9 innings to break Bob Feller's single-game American League strikeout record of 18. Those 19 strikeouts also tied the major league record held by Steve Carlton and Tom Seaver.

Tom phoned and congratulated me. "You know, Tom," I kidded, "I let Rick Burleson hit the last pitch so that the name Seaver wouldn't be knocked out of the record book."

"That was nice of you," Tom kidded back. "I always appreciate a favor from an old buddy."

What had actually happened in that at bat was that Burleson had fouled off a third strike. Then he hit a fly-ball out. If I had gotten that pitch by him I would have jumped on the phone to call Tom before he had a chance to call me.

On August 20, 1974, I struck out 19 batters against Detroit in 11 innings. Then on June 8, 1977, I got 19 K's in 10 innings against the Toronto Blue Jays. So four of the seven 19-strikeout games were pitched by me. I also had the good fortune to be there to see the ones pitched by Tom Seaver and Steve Carlton when I was playing for the Mets.

Tom's 19 strikeouts came against the San Diego Padres at Shea Stadium in 1970. He struck out the last 10 guys he faced. It was a phenomenal feat, probably the most over-powering pitching performance I've ever seen in one game. It was in the afternoon with the shadows coming in, but none of that took anything away from Tom's performance. He had exceptionally good stuff that day.

Carlton's 19-strikeout game took place in 1969. Carlton was on his game. So was Ron Swoboda, who hit two home runs off Steve. And although Carlton got 19 K's, he also lost the game.

In 1986 Roger Clemens of the Red Sox struck out 20 in a game. That knocked Seaver, Carlton, and me out of that spot in the record book. It didn't bother me any. I've always had the attitude about all my records that since I was able to accomplish them, there's no reason why someone else shouldn't be able to come along and break them. What Roger Clemens did is a perfect example of that.

One of my biggest kicks as a pitcher has been the challenge of going head to head with the true power hitters, the guys able to beat you with one swing.

On that list I include, from the right side, Orlando Cepeda, Dick Allen, Mike Schmidt, Pedro Guerrero, and Jack Clark, and from the left side, Willie Stargell, Willie McCovey, Reggie Jackson, Dave Parker, and Darryl Strawberry.

Dick Allen was one of those I always enjoyed pitching against. It was a challenge because he was a quality hitter, knew the strike zone, and wouldn't help a pitcher out by going for a bad pitch.

Once when we were playing against the Chicago White Sox and it was late in the game and it had pretty much been decided, Dick Allen was the batter.

I said, "Dick, nothing but fastballs."

"What's that?" he called back.

I said it again. "Nothing but fastballs."

"Then let's get it on." Dick waved his bat.

The game wasn't in jeopardy—I'd never do something like that when a game is on the line—but I still don't know what possessed me to talk to Allen like that. Maybe it was because Dick was a top fastball hitter and a player who loved a challenge.

I threw about ten pitches to him, all of them in the 95-plus-mile-per-hour range. But Dick had great bat speed, and he kept fouling off pitch after pitch. We had quite a battle for a time there. Finally I got him out on a fly ball to right field.

I had the same kind of encounter one time with Reggie Jackson. I called my catcher, Elly Rodriguez, out and told him, "Tell Reggie I'm throwing him nothing but heat." Elly told him. Reggie looked out at me and nodded. The final result of all of that depends on whom you talk to. I say Reggie was out on a fly ball to left. Reggie says he hit a line drive to left. Reggie has never been one who likes to be outdone.

In a game in 1979 I struck out the first two hitters in an inning and then Reggie came to bat. I got two strikes on him and decided I wasn't going to waste a pitch. I figured I'd throw the ball past him as hard as I could and strike him out. I threw the ball past Reggie for strike three, and I hurt my elbow and ended up walking off the mound. I wound up not pitching for ten days.

Sometimes those big power hitters were less of a challenge to me than I was to myself. In that case with Reggie I was my own worst enemy.

In my last start of 1974, on September 28 against the third-place Minnesota Twins, I pitched my third no-hitter. Of the five no-hitters I've pitched, that one is the least vivid in my memory.

Ruth and Reid had already gone back to Texas and my thoughts were on getting packed up, closing down the house, and heading for home. It was a lost season, a down time. The whole team was just finishing the year up. Those last six weeks of the season had been tedious. We were completely out of the pennant race. A lot of our players felt very insecure on the ball club. We always had a big turnover in personnel. With Dick Williams having taken over as manager, there was even more insecurity. Now it was the end of the season, and some guys knew they would not be back.

At that time Minnesota was the best-hitting team in the American League, with top hitters like Rod Carew, Larry Hisle, and Tony Oliva, so I knew I had some tough pitching to do. I got off to a real good start. My first seven pitches were strikes. I struck out the side in each of the first two innings.

I could feel the extra hop on my fastball, so I told my catcher, Tom Egan, "I think I'll let it all hang out. What have I got to lose?"

Although it was one of those games where I didn't have good command of my stuff—I was behind in the count a lot and threw a lot of pitches—I had tremendous velocity on the fastball and a hard-breaking curve.

In the ninth I got the first two batters, and then Minnesota sent up Harmon Killebrew to pinch-hit. The crowd booed. I didn't feel so good about seeing that big guy either. I pitched carefully to Killebrew, not wanting to give a hitter of his stature a pitch he could pull. I wound up walking him. Then I went to a 2–2 count on Eric Soderholm and threw him a high fastball. He swung late, missed, and the game was over.

I wound up walking 8 batters, 7 in the first 5 innings— and striking out 15 batters in the game. I finished with 367 strikeouts that year, the third year in a row I struck out 300 or more batters. That no-hitter gave me 22 wins for a last-place team, and it was the eleventh time I'd held the opposition to four or fewer hits in a game that year.

My individual stats were good—Ferguson Jenkins and Catfish Hunter were the only American League pitchers who won more games than me. I was first in strikeouts and innings pitched, fourth in complete games, first in fewest hits per nine innings, and right up there with the ERA leaders. But the Angels were at the bottom of the heap. We finished with the worst record in the American League— 22 games behind Oakland in the West. I wished I could have done even more for the team and the fans.

WHITEY HERZOG:

Nolan did enough. In his first three years with the Angels he won 62 games and struck out a mind-boggling 1,079 batters.

He was a workhorse on a team that couldn't hit and couldn't field. Some idiots called him a .500 pitcher. Crap—he was a .500 pitcher on a .350 horseshit team.

RON LUCIANO:

He's been called a .500 pitcher by people who know nothing. Ask Amos Otis, who had Ryanitis, who was scared to get in there and bat against Nolan, if Ryan was a .500 pitcher. Ask Reggie Jackson. Ask Don Baylor. Ask Rod Carew. Nolan is not a .500 pitcher. He's a dominator.

Nolan's got five years to wait to get into the Hall of Fame after he retires, but there's no question that he's going to make it. I'm going to love to go to Cooperstown and listen to his speech. He'll walk around the podium a few times, the way he walks around the mound. He'll thank everybody. The whole speech probably won't be more than three words.

Throughout spring training of 1975 I was bothered by all kinds of minor nagging injuries, from pulled calf muscles to a hamstring. When the season began, I suffered twice through bad groin pulls. Up to that time in my career I had always been free of any real physical problems.

In the middle of April we were in Minnesota, and I woke up in the morning and felt a terrible ache in my arm. I looked at my elbow and it was swollen. It was a frightening feeling—one that all pitchers dread. I rushed down to the ballpark and got somebody to catch me. It was a case of my just checking to see if I could throw even at half speed. I could, but I knew I'd have to get checked out further. I realized then that I might have been putting a strain on my arm, altering my delivery to pitch through the nagging injuries.

Later on, after the team doctor took some X rays, it turned out that I had bone chips in my elbow. But I was told not to worry, that the chips were from an old injury and that things would work out all right. I wondered.

I moved through the season, winning six of my first seven decisions. My elbow bothered me a lot and throbbed like a bad tooth. It was only when I got loose that the arm and the elbow felt a bit better.

Then on June 1 something happened that I thought was unbelievable. Against Baltimore at Anaheim, before 18,942 fans in my twelfth start of the season, pitching in pain, pitching without my best stuff, I got my fourth no-hitter. I struck out nine and walked four. We won the game, 1–0.

I started to think some about the no-hitter in the fifth and sixth innings, but I never had the feeling it was happening. I remembered that ten times before as an Angel I had gone to the seventh inning looking for a no-hitter only to come up empty.

In the last three innings the crowd was on its feet cheering every pitch I made. But even going into the ninth inning, I had my doubts about the no-hitter. Baltimore had so many good hitters that you had to go out by out. And in the ninth inning they had three of their toughest due up: Al Bumbry, Tommy Davis, and Bobby Grich.

I got Bumbry on a fly ball to left. Davis grounded out to

second baseman Jerry Remy, who was just a rookie then and nervous as a new mother cat about possibly screwing up my chance for the no-hitter.

The last out of that game was the one everyone talked about. I worked Bobby Grich, a real tough out, to a 2–2 count. He had fouled two fastballs straight back, so I knew he was sitting on my fastball. I knew that if I got my change-up over, I would have him, because Grich and everybody else in that ballpark expected one thing and one thing only: heat. I threw him the change-up, froze him, and got him on a called strike three.

BOBBY GRICH:

> Damn right he fooled me. I wasn't thinking anything but looking for the ball up there, swinging for a home run. But I didn't expect a change-up. Ryan got it in a perfect spot, low and away.

When I got Grich on the change-up, it meant that I had come a long way. I had come to the majors as a one-pitch pitcher. Then I had developed an outstanding curveball, but it was inconsistent. I had been working on a change-up, but it was inconsistent, too. I was wild with it and threw it way too hard. I hadn't come up with a way of throwing it where the velocity was what it should be—10 mph less than my fastball.

But in that particular situation I thought it was the pitch to throw. Now, if Grich had hit the ball out of the ballpark, I probably would be saying that it was the worst pitch I'd ever thrown.

Of all my no-hitters, that one was the most satisfying. It was a pure pitching performance. There wasn't one difficult play in the whole game. In the second no-hitter, I had the most raw ability, but that fourth one showed my considerable transition from a thrower to a pitcher.

Ruth always sits behind home plate in the box seats when she comes to the games. And she sat through that no-hitter —the first one of mine she ever saw in person—counting every strike, counting every out. Ruth was the only one who really knew how much I had been hurting, how unexpected that no-hitter was.

I told the press after the game that I had been lucky, that I really hadn't had good stuff. They didn't believe me. I guess what I was saying seemed to them to be kind of crazy or a case of false modesty. I also told them that it was nice to have the recognition but that it didn't change my thinking about the way I pitched. I just don't go into games thinking no-hitter. I don't place that much emphasis on the single accomplishment. I don't think they believed that either, but it was the truth.

There was lots of celebrating afterward and many bottles of champagne in the clubhouse. I turned down a glass of champagne but did have a beer, which I enjoy occasionally. I decided the best way to celebrate was to go out for a quiet dinner with Ruth, and that's what we did.

That fourth no-hitter tied me with Sandy Koufax, and accomplishing that and having broken Sandy's season strikeout record were the two biggest events in my career up till then. That was because, as I've said, I was a big Sandy Koufax fan. I never compared myself to him—but anytime you surpass or accomplish what your idol accomplished, that has special meaning for you.

When I broke his season strikeout record, Sandy sent me a telegram. Then when I tied his record for no-hitters I received another telegram from him offering congratulations.

I had first come into contact with Sandy when I was with the Mets and he was doing the "Game of the Week" for NBC. When I saw him back then at Shea Stadium, I made it a point to go up to him and introduce myself. I was just another young kid struggling to stay in the big leagues and he was one of the greatest pitchers there ever was. He didn't know me from Adam. Yet he was very polite, a real gentleman.

I have often thought about how amazing it has been that the pitcher I admired most as a high school kid would have his great strikeout records broken by me. Through the years I've met so many people in baseball, and Sandy still remains one of those I admire the most for what he accomplished on the field and the way he conducts himself in his life.

Those first couple of years in the seventies, attendance in baseball was in decline. In Anaheim we drew under a million fans in 1971 and 1972. We weren't putting a good product on the field. So the Angels did what any other club would have done: they took any positive thing they had and they promoted it as much as possible. I was used as a kind of marquee attraction. It was "Nolan Ryan versus New York Yankees," or "Nolan Ryan pitches Thursday." I certainly didn't have any problem with that.

RON LUCIANO:

Nolan drew crowds to Anaheim like crazy. I'd come in to umpire a series and there'd be 6,000 fans there for three nights in a row. Then on the fourth night there'd be 40,000. Nolan was pitching.

Home run hitters draw like that. Dwight Gooden does it with the Mets now, but he's in New York City with all those people there. Fernando does it with the Dodgers, but he's in L.A. Try to do something like that in Anaheim.

Nolan awed people. He had them spellbound. You could hear the hushes. Normally at Anaheim they had these beach balls which they'd throw and carry around in the stands. But not when Nolan pitched. Those fans hung on every pitch. The concession stands did less business.

The ballplayers on the Angel team were scared to death that they would make an error while he was out there, not because they would let Nolan down but because they knew they might be keeping him out of the record book. Every time he was out there pitching there was the potential for a no-hitter or another record of some kind.

Before my first start after I had pitched the fourth no-hitter, there was more hype, more promotion, and more attention paid to me than ever before. All kinds of report-ers came into Anaheim from around the country to cover the game. The sense of drama was doubled—now not only were they all talking about my chances of pitching back-to-back no-hitters to tie Johnny Vander Meer, they were also doing a lot of talking about my having a shot at pitching a fifth no-hitter, something no one had ever done before.

Almost 30,000 fans, a lot for Anaheim Stadium, were there when I went out to pitch against Milwaukee looking for a miracle to happen. My arm tingled, and my stuff was not the best, but the crowd was into the game and so was I.

The first three innings went by, and I had held Milwau-kee hitless. My velocity wasn't there, but I worked the hitters. Through the fifth, I still had the no-hitter. And with each pitch, each out, the fans seemed to be cheering more. I got the first two batters in the sixth inning. At that point I was counting. Ten more outs. Ten more outs, I told myself.

Then Hank Aaron punched one through the infield over second base. That ended it. A big groan rolled through the ballpark, and, standing there on the mound, I groaned, too. I finished that game with a two-hit shutout, making my record 10–3, with five shutouts. I was doing well despite the bad elbow and losing the no-hitter.

When reporters asked me afterward how I felt, I got off a pretty good line: "Well, now Henry Aaron will have some-thing to say about his career highlights, that he was the one who broke up Nolan Ryan's try for back-to-back no-hitters that would have given Ryan five for his career."

I was on top of the mountain, so I joked around. My

record was 10–3, and 5 of my wins had come through shutouts. I had a two-year contract with the Angels at $125,000 a season, so I was feeling good, maybe too good.

Then it all turned around, and suddenly I had a big fall. My elbow trouble came back, and I was knocked out in three straight starts. I was really roughed up.

That was a tough thing for me to handle, since I had been pitching so well, totally dominating the hitters. Now the shoe was on the other foot. A lot of those hitters who didn't look forward to facing me now just couldn't wait to get in there against me.

Then, on top of the arm trouble, I suffered a pretty bad groin pull. The only positive thing about it was that I was able to tell the writers who covered the Angels that my arm was all right but my pitching motion had been thrown off by the groin problem.

The truth of the matter, though, was that I was going through a crisis—something that every pitcher dreads. In order to brush my teeth or comb my hair I had to bend my head down: that's how bad the pain in the arm was. It was a frightening time. I truly believed that my career was coming to its end.

The reporters covering the Angels had their job to do and it included writing about me. When they couldn't get the facts, they speculated. Some of them speculated a little too much. Some of them didn't believe in letting the truth get in the way of a good story.

A couple of articles appeared in the newspapers that

claimed I was burned out, that I had given up on the team and the season, that I had lost interest in baseball.

It was a situation that made me acutely aware of the power of the press to shape an image, any kind of image they wanted. Some of what those sportswriters were saying about me was a bunch of untruths, and I let them know it.

Then I did a foolish thing. I went into a shell. When games ended I hid out in the shower room or the trainers' room. It was a case of my just not feeling like talking to the reporters and answering the same questions: "How's your arm? Are you feeling any better?"

Stories also appeared in the newspapers that claimed that I wasn't talking to my teammates. Those stories were a pack of lies. I usually didn't do that much talking anyway. I've never been one of those who made small talk or roughhoused around or partied with the boys. I usually stayed to myself, roomed alone, kept to my own business. Now my normal behavior was being reported as exclusionary.

I didn't exclude myself from the team. I just pulled in a bit more. The Angels were going bad and so was I. Since I wasn't helping them, I felt as if I was letting them down.

My ineffectiveness reached a point where I lost eight straight games. Finally, in late August, the pain in my elbow became so bad that I just stopped pitching. My record was 14–12 and I had 186 strikeouts in 198 innings.

After a lot of talk, meetings, and checkups, I consented to have an operation. On August 23, 1975, the operation was performed. It was a very simple procedure that removed four pieces of calcium that were rubbing inside the joint of my elbow, making for all the pain and stiffness. I had a splint on my elbow until mid-October. And all through that off-season I wondered about my future and what it would be like to throw again.

On January 21, 1976, ten days before my twenty-ninth birthday, our second son was born. Ruth and I named him Nolan Reese—Reese after Jimmy Reese. We were now a family of four. Just about the time Reese was born, I started to throw the ball again. I was pretty relieved that I felt no pain. I didn't throw hard but just limbered up my arm. I was confident that I could come back to what I had been as a pitcher, and I couldn't wait for spring training to begin so I could start all over again.

Anyone looking at my record for 1976 would probably say that I had a bad year. Actually it was a bad year that turned out in the end to be a very good year for me in a season where all the events seemed to just run together.

One thing I recall quite vividly is a scene that took place on the team bus in late July. We were about twenty games under .500, and the mood on the Angels was very much down. Dick Williams was more irritated than usual, and so were most of the players.

One of our veterans, Bill Melton, challenged Dick Williams. They were going at it with a lot of obscenity. Some of the other players got into it by blasting the volume on their portable radios. It was one of the more ugly scenes I've seen in my time in baseball.

Melton was suspended, but Williams was fired by Harry Dalton. Norm Sherry, who had been our pitching coach, replaced Dick. That change had a pretty positive effect on the team. Under Norm, the Angels had a winning record and wound up the year in fourth place, fourteen games behind Kansas City.

In a way, what happened to the Angels echoed my own season. I was 6–9 with a 3.84 ERA the first half of '76 and then 11–9 with a 2.98 ERA the second half. I pitched the most shutouts in the league, was among the leaders in complete games, and struck out 327 batters in 284 innings. One of those strikeouts was on August 31 against Ron LeFlore of the Detroit Tigers. It was my 2,000th career strikeout. The last ten weeks of the season I pitched four three-hitters.

The 1976 season was a kind of comeback time for me. What was most satisfying as the year ended was that I knew my arm had come around and I had about as much strength in it as I had before that elbow trouble.

At the start of 1977 I signed a three-year contract with the Angels. I looked forward to my future there with the ball club. I had high expectations and felt that we could be competitive. Over the winter, Harry Dalton had signed free agents Joe Rudi, Bobby Grich, and Don Baylor—three proven hitters—to long-term contracts for nearly $5 million. Those three guys were in the top 15 percent of players in the American League. I had done a lot of tough pitching against them. Now I was happy to have them on our side. We had been getting by with a popgun offense for too long. Now we would have some hitters. There was a lot of hype. The Angel fans felt we just might have bought ourselves a pennant.

When I went to spring training, Ruth stayed back home in Alvin because she was expecting our third child. I was in Tucson playing an exhibition game against Cleveland. Ruth called after the game and said she was due to have the baby within twenty-four hours. I flew to Texas to be there with her. Our daughter, Wendy, was born March 22, 1977. We were delighted to have a baby girl after the two boys. Much as I hated to leave Ruth and the kids, I had an obligation to the team. So a few days after Wendy was born, I flew back to Palm Springs to join the club and continue spring training.

Up to that time when I was on the Angels, we always lived in rented houses. When the 1977 season began, with the new three-year contract and the new baby, we decided to purchase a house in Villa Park, California, a nice residential community. I bought and furnished the house myself while Ruth was in Texas with the kids. They all moved out there around June 1. I never thought of myself as an interior decorator, but Ruth seemed satisfied with what I had done when she came out. We both felt that owning our own home gave us roots in Southern California.

With a new contract and a new baby and the potential power of the new free agents behind me, I had a lot of motivation that '77 season. I wound up with one of my best years with the Angels, leading the league in strikeouts, complete games, and fewest hits and most strikeouts per nine innings. I won 19 games and allowed 100 fewer hits than innings pitched. *The Sporting News* voted me the American League Pitcher of the Year, and that pleased me.

Frank Tanana also had a very good year for the Angels, winning fifteen games and leading the league in ERA. Frank would make the biggest overall transition of anyone I ever saw in baseball. In 1973 he had come to the Angels as a playboy, a party-going free-spirited bachelor. Frank had a real live fastball and an excellent curve. Then he had arm trouble. He lost his velocity and became a finesse pitcher with control. His life-style also changed when he got married and became a born-again Christian. Now Frank's with the Tigers in his hometown of Detroit and he continues to be an effective pitcher. I've always thought Frank was a good example of the potential that people have for growth and change, and of the value of faith in an individual's life.

However, even with Frank Tanana and me having such good years in 1977, the Angels never clicked as a ball club. We didn't have that spark as a team unit. During the season Dave Garcia replaced Norm Sherry, who had replaced Dick Williams as manager. With the changes in managers and the fact that it takes a while for a team to come together and fit in, the team was in flux. If only one new free agent had been added to the team, he could have been eased into the chemistry of the club. But as it was, there were too many new faces coming and going, which made for a lot of adjustments. The lack of stability affected our performance.

Baylor, Rudi, and Grich as a group didn't contribute as much as everyone had expected. Grich was hobbled by injuries. Baylor, who I remain good friends with and who is a natural team leader, hit twenty-five home runs and helped us the most. Joe Rudi was a ballplayer's ballplayer. He didn't have exceptional talent, but he made the most of what he had. But being a free agent was a bigger adjustment for Joe than for Baylor and Grich. Don had made two previous stops with other teams and could adjust to different situations easily. He had also moved from Baltimore to Oakland only the year before. Grich was comfortable in Anaheim, since he lived in Long Beach, and had gone to college in California. On the other hand, Rudi's big contract created pressures and distractions for him. Most of the time he was with us, he was afflicted by leg injuries, and he also got his hand banged up when he was hit by a pitch from Nelson Briles.

Prior to Rudi's getting hit, there had been a few beanball incidents, and Commissioner Bowie Kuhn had sent out a memo that said if there was any retaliation by a pitcher, he would be thrown out of the game, fined, and suspended indefinitely. All the time Gene Autry owned the Angels, his attitude and presence never changed. He was the big constant at Anaheim. I'm sure he was frustrated at never seeing his team get into the World Series, but he never let his desire and his hopes dim. After Joe Rudi got hit, Gene called a team meeting. It was the first time that he ever ran one himself.

"I want you all to know," he told us, "that I don't care what Bowie Kuhn said. It isn't the commissioner's $5 million that was spent on free agents. It's my $5 million. I want you pitchers on the Angels to protect our hitters. I'll be damned if I'm going to let our people get pushed around. If any of you pitchers retaliate to protect a teammate and you get suspended, you can be damn sure I'll pay the fine and I'll pay your salary. So you have nothing to worry about."

That was the kind of owner Gene Autry was. That was the kind of man Gene Autry was. He knew how to take care of his players, and he knew how to help morale. And our team needed all the morale-boosting it could get after we finished that '77 season in fifth place, twenty-eight games behind Whitey Herzog's Kansas City Royals.

When the season ended, Harry Dalton was fired. On October 27, 1977, Buzzie Bavasi was appointed to replace him. I was unhappy to see Harry leave the Angels. We were friends. We had spent many good times together talking baseball, and Harry respected my views. Harry had made a lot of trades, signed free agents, and tried everything he could think of to try and turn our Angel ball club around. But it just didn't work. He moved on to Milwaukee.

During that 1977 season I was involved in another bit of a fracas with Billy Martin and Jim Palmer, who some people called my old sparring partners. Frank Tanana had been picked for the All-Star team but had some trouble with his arm, so he couldn't pitch. The day before the game was to be played I received a phone call and was asked to take Frank's place on the team. I turned them down. I had made plans to spend the three-day All-Star break with my family and didn't want to change them. I didn't want to fly all the way across the country from California to New York, where the game was being played. I also had been on the team before and thought it was a good opportunity for them to give some other deserving pitcher a chance.

It was inaccurately reported that I did not want to be on the All-Star team because Billy Martin was the manager. It had nothing to do with Billy or Jim Palmer, who ended up as the American League starter and did a lot of complaining about me. I never could figure out why they both took exception to my actions, but they always seemed to have something to say about me.

I started the '78 season on track, giving up no runs in four of my first six starts, but had only a 2–1 record to show for it. I struck out fifteen against Seattle in late April and pitched a one-hitter against Cleveland on May 5. I don't think I've ever thrown better that early in the season. Usually I don't throw that well until June.

On June 1 Jim Fregosi took over as manager. He was the seventh manager I had in my time at Anaheim. I always anticipated that Jim would manage the Angels at some point because when he was traded for me, he had been the most popular and consistent player they ever had. It was also common knowledge that Fregosi was a personal friend of Gene Autry's.

After he left the Angels and went to the Mets, Fregosi didn't perform at the level New York anticipated, and he basically became a utility player. I didn't know him. And I didn't know whether he had any animosity against me because of the success and popularity I had gained with the Angels. But we went on to develop a good relationship, and I considered him a good manager. He was what I would call a player's manager. You could go in and talk to him.

Soon after Fregosi joined the club, I did a kind of foolish thing. We had a catcher by the name of Terry Humphrey, and the players on the Angels were riding him about how slow he was. I got talked into having a race with Terry in the outfield. I beat him, but I pulled a hamstring in my left leg and was on the disabled list from June 14 to July 5. When I came off the DL, I won only once in my next seven starts because I had a lot of trouble getting my rhythm back.

On August 12, 1978, I recorded career strikeout number 2,500. It was against Buddy Bell of the Cleveland Indians, and just for a moment there my mind drifted back to sitting in the dugout back in 1969 with Tom Seaver, watching Jim Bunning pitch at Shea Stadium.

Just when I was finally getting untracked from my first stay on the DL while I was with the Angels, I suffered a rib separation on my left side and was on the disabled list again from August 20 to September 6. I was thirty-one years old then, and I guess my body was going through some physical transitions.

During the previous winter Lyman Bostock had signed with the Angels as a free agent. He had been a .300 hitter his first three seasons with the Minnesota Twins. Early in the season Lyman was pressing too much, which caused him to get off to a real bad start. Around the first of June he was so frustrated and disappointed in himself that he offered to give back part of his salary. We all told him to just ease up, that his numbers would come. And they did. Lyman was batting close to .300 on September 23, 1978, when our team finished playing a day game against the White Sox in Chicago.

After the game, as the story was reported to me, Lyman drove in a car with his wife and his uncle to Gary, Indiana. Lyman's uncle was dating a girl who they picked up. Then, as the story goes, some kind of serious domestic quarrel developed over that girl. There was a car chase all over Gary, Indiana. Lyman, in the backseat of the car and an innocent party to the whole thing, wound up getting shot in the head and killed. He was only twenty-seven years old.

Lyman had been with us just that one year, but all the Angel players had gotten to know him and like him because he was a personable guy who played hard. His death devastated our ball club and left us all in shock. I remember pitching the day after his death, and the furthest thing from my mind was whether we'd win or lose. What happened to Lyman was kind of the final blow in a year that had begun with high hopes for a pennant for the Angels and ended with us finishing in second place, five games behind Kansas City.

As it was, the Angels won 87 games, their most ever to that point. Their second-place finish was the highest in their history till then. Although that '78 season was a pretty successful one for the Angels, it was a frustrating one for me. I wound up the season with a 10–13 record—my worst won and lost record since 1971, when I was 10–14 with the New York Mets. It was small consolation that even with my injuries and missing about half a dozen starts, I was able four times to strike out 13 or more in a game and to finish with 260 strikeouts for the season, to lead the American League once again in that category.

Through seven seasons with the California Angels, I had pitched four no-hitters, six one-hitters, thirteen two-hitters, twenty-two three-hitters, and thirty-five shutouts. During my time at Anaheim, I had averaged 10.07 strikeouts per game and now had 2,686 career strikeouts, placing me eighth on the all-time list. My 1,079 strikeouts from 1972 to 1974 were a major league record for three straight seasons that broke the old mark of 922, set by Sandy Koufax from 1964 to 1966.

One of the stats I was proudest of was my 95–2 record in games I pitched where the Angels had the lead after seven innings. That stat showed I was capable of shutting the door on the opposition, that I had the endurance to finish games.

Over the winter of 1978–79 the Angels traded for Rod Carew. He seemed to be the added ingredient we needed

Jimmy Reese—a grand guy
and a good buddy. (PHOTO
COURTESY NOLAN RYAN)

The final pitch in my first no-
hitter, May 15, 1973, against
Kansas City. (PHOTO ERNIE
SCHWARCK/UPI)

Giving it all I had to get my twentieth win on September 23, 1973.
(AP/WORLDWIDE PHOTO)

Savoring the moment after setting the all-time season strikeout record in 1973. (UPI PHOTO)

The old baseball field I played on in Alvin—named for me in the fall of 1973 after I pitched the two no-hitters. (PHOTO COURTESY NOLAN RYAN)

Leaving the field after the
third no-hitter, September 28,
1974, against Minnesota.
(PHOTO COURTESY NOLAN RYAN)

Here I am, getting ready to
smoke it. (PHOTO BY HAROLD
ISRAEL/GULF PHOTO)

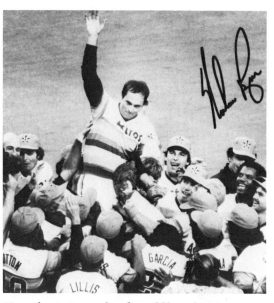

Face to face with my idol, Sandy Koufax. (PHOTO BY JOEL DRAUT/THE HOUSTON *POST*)

Here I've just completed my fifth no-hitter, September 26, 1981. I think that fifth one was the most satisfying of them all. (PHOTO BY JOEL DRAUT/THE HOUSTON *POST*)

Since the fifth no-hitter broke the record, it generated a lot of media attention and excitement. (PHOTO COURTESY ALVIN *SUN*)

With Ruth and very happy after getting my 4,000th strike-out. (PHOTO © F. CARTER SMITH)

One of my memorable moments: strikeout number 4,000 on July 11, 1985. That's Danny Heep of the Mets. (PHOTO COURTESY NOLAN RYAN)

Just a couple of Texans in the Houston dugout—that's Vice-President George Bush in civilian clothes. (PHOTO BY DAVE VALDEZ/THE WHITE HOUSE)

A father's pride—a 1987 shot. Reid is on my right and Reese on my left. (PHOTO COURTESY NOLAN RYAN)

A family portrait—at home at the ranch in Alvin. (PHOTO © 1987 JANICE RUBIN)

to get us over the hump. Rod was one of the best hitters I've ever seen. He had great bat control, could bunt with two strikes on him, and could use the whole ballpark as a hitter. He made adjustments all the time so you couldn't pitch him one way. Even though I struck him out more times than I did any other American League hitter, he was a tough out. People later kidded him that he came to California so he wouldn't have to hit against me. But the reason Rod struck out so much against me was that he was a leadoff hitter in our division, which meant that he faced me four or five times a game. What also should be mentioned is that he hit .300 off me. Rod and his family became our neighbors in Villa Park, and I got to know him, his wife, Marilyn, and their kids very well. Rod and I would ride to the ballpark together. Because he was quiet and stayed to himself, he was misunderstood. But Rod was a very dedicated player.

In 1967 Rod Carew was the Rookie of the Year with the Minnesota Twins. All through the years he was really the constant there. Harmon Killebrew had retired. Tony Oliva had retired. And Rod was to Minnesota what I was to the Angels. People thought of "Rod Carew of the Minnesota Twins" and "Nolan Ryan of the California Angels."

Going into the 1979 season, many people viewed me as the constant on the California Angels, the player who gave the team its identity, the only one left from the 1972 team. I'd been there the longest, been there through the lean years, and I was ready for winning. I felt that I'd developed a special relationship with the fans at Anaheim Stadium.

That was my baseball home, much more so than Shea Stadium ever was.

Since I was going into the final and option year of a three-year contract at $300,000 a year, I wrote a letter to Buzzie Bavasi in January of 1979, telling him that I had no intentions of going into free agency and that I wanted to sign a contract extension. I asked for a three-year contract at $400,000 a year with a $200,000 bonus for signing. The whole package would have come out to $1.4 million for three years.

When Buzzie had replaced Harry Dalton, the Angels had started to enjoy more success, to put things together. As in most baseball instances, when a new guy comes in, he usually reaps the benefits if a team is doing well. And that seemed to be the case with Buzzie. I received a letter from him which said that he didn't believe in renegotiating contracts before they expired or in contract extensions. He said that we could discuss it all at the end of the year.

During all those seasons I was with the Angels, Gene Autry was there in the clubhouse and with the team strictly as a fan. Only once, the time when Joe Rudi got hurt, did he interfere with baseball matters. Gene never looked for public exposure. He'd gotten all the publicity he needed when he was a movie star. His motivation was different from that of a lot of owners of baseball teams, who buy a club to get exposure. Gene hired people to handle the baseball aspects of the team. As a player, you understood that and never talked money to him. And he never discussed money matters with any of the Angels. So even though I was good friends with Gene and we liked each other a lot, I knew what the deal was. I never approached him when I had my differences with Buzzie Bavasi. Gene has since told me that was the one time he should have gotten involved. And looking back on it, maybe I should have gotten together with him and talked.

As the 1979 season got under way, there were a few things that appeared in the press attributed to Buzzie Bavasi that just showed we were not compatible. Ruth and I and the kids were very comfortable in Southern California, and as I said, the Angels were my team. But I knew as long as Buzzie was with the club, it would be an unpleasant situation for me. I decided that I'd file for free agency after the season.

Throughout my career, I had never had an agent. I always handled my own contract negotiations. However, since I was thinking of filing for free agency, I began to think I could use some professional help and retained Dick Moss, who had been the legal counsel for the Players Association.

I thought that my unsettled status with the Angels would be the paramount thing on my mind that whole baseball season. But on May 9, 1979, an event took place that was to cause me far greater anxiety.

I was in Fenway Park in Boston when I got a call from Ruth during the game. It was one of those things all players dread: an unexpected call from home.

"Don't be alarmed, Nolan," Ruth began. "Reid's had an accident, but I think he's okay."

"What happened?"

"He was hit by a car," Ruth continued in her calm, soft-spoken voice. "The doctors think it's no more than a broken leg. Nothing serious. It looks like there are no internal injuries because all Reid's vital signs are good. Still, they want to take tests to be sure." She hesitated. "Nolan," she said, "I need you. When can you get here?"

"I'm leaving right now."

I left the ballpark, got on a plane, and flew home. I was there by morning. Then I found out what had happened. Reid, who was seven years old then, had just gotten his uniform shirt for the little baseball team he was going to play on. He was so proud of it, he went across the street to show it off to his friends.

There were two brothers who lived down the street who were older than the rest of the kids on the block. They had a tendency to be bullies and would antagonize the little kids. When they saw Reid in his new shirt, they came over and started teasing him, threatening to tear his shirt off.

He didn't want any part of that and started darting across the street to go home. Just at that moment a girl was driving down the block in her automobile, and a tree on the corner blocked her view. She went right into Reid.

Ruth was standing in the front yard, talking to Marilyn Carew. They saw Reid being hit and ran out into the street. It seemed like Reid was all right except for the broken leg. Ruth called the paramedics, and they rushed him to Orange County Children's Hospital.

By the time I got there, Reid's condition had worsened.

He was in extreme pain. They had to do some exploratory surgery to see what the problem was. It turned out that he did have internal injuries after all. He had to undergo two operations. When it was all over, Reid had lost one of his kidneys and his spleen. He had to spend ninety days in traction for the broken femur.

That began the long summer of 1979. Because of Reid's condition I wouldn't go on road trips with the Angels until the day before I was scheduled to pitch. I'd stay back and help Ruth manage the hospital visits and taking care of the two babies—Reese, who was three, and Wendy, who was two. I'd get up and go to the hospital in the morning. When the team was home, Ruth would go to the hospital early each morning, and then I would go over and relieve her around 11 A.M. I would stay until I had to go to the ballpark at 4 P.M. Ruth would then come back and stay until Reid was asleep. Our summer was pretty well spent spelling each other at the hospital.

It was an agonizing time, a stressful period in our lives, but all of that trouble brought us closer together as a family. I think it also opened our eyes even more to a lot of the terrible problems that people have in the world.

We spent so much time at that hospital. And I saw so many sick kids, terminally ill kids, kids who had just had bad accidents. A lot of those kids were baseball fans. I signed autographs and baseballs and visited with them and did whatever I could to cheer them up.

Reid came through that ordeal and he's a healthy kid, but for a lot of other kids things don't work out. That experience intensified what I'd always felt: that if there's something I can do to help make the lives of young people better and easier, then I'll do it.

Ruth and I have always been involved with Little League. I've also set up a scholarship fund at Alvin Community College, where we've raised over $100,000 to try and improve the program there and give the kids in the area an opportunity to play baseball and further their education.

And just recently, in 1987, I got involved with Whitehall Laboratories' Advil program in conjunction with the National Association for Sports and Physical Education. It's an awareness program to make young people more educated about physical fitness. We've developed materials on how to handle stress and emergencies, how kids should prepare to take part in sports, how they should recognize injuries and not play through them.

I was the starting pitcher for the American League in the 1979 All-Star Game in Seattle. Just around that time I pitched in a game that I still think about now and then. After all the games I've pitched in my career, so many of them just seem to blend together. But that game I still remember vividly, and whenever I come into contact with the guys who were with me on the Angels then, we get to reminiscing about that game. It was against the New York Yankees, on national TV, and before a sellout crowd of 41,805.

The game had a five-fifteen start with the sun still up in midsummer in Anaheim, and that was a real pretty time of day in Southern California. It wasn't too bad a time for a thirty-two-year-old fastball pitcher like me to ply his trade either. The Yankees knew it, too. During batting practice New York catcher Thurman Munson sent a message to me through my teammate pitcher Jim Barr.

"You can tell Nolan that it won't matter what the light's like at five o'clock," Munson said. "I can't hit him at eight o'clock either."

Shutting out the Red Sox on six hits four nights earlier, I had thrown a lot of pitches, so I was a little tired going up against the Yankees. But seeing those pinstripes gave me a little extra charge. After five innings I had struck out Graig Nettles, Lou Piniella, Bucky Dent, Bobby Murcer, and Thurman Munson. I had also given up no runs and no hits.

The crowd was into it from the fifth inning on, giving me a lot of applause each time I left the mound after giving up no hits. In the seventh inning I got Nettles and Piniella again on strikeouts. We led 3–0. I've never been that big on stats, but I knew I had won 105 of 110 games when I was leading after seven innings. I bore down—the win was primary in my mind. The no-hitter, I knew, would take care of itself; I had to just concentrate pitch by pitch.

In the eighth, Chris Chambliss led off for the Yankees and hit a fly ball to deep center field. Rick Miller, my old sparring partner, caught the ball. Now I was counting along with everyone else in Anaheim Stadium. I needed five more outs for the no-hitter.

Jim Spencer, the Yankee DH, was next. He tagged a sinking liner to center field. Rick Miller came rushing in, fell to his knees, got his glove on the ball, but it bounced off and rolled away from him. I couldn't tell whether it was a hit or an error. It was a tough play. Rick was a good fielder, but it was his first game back off the disabled list. He had a hand problem. Whether that affected his handling of the ball or not I don't know.

The scoreboard immediately flashed "E." Dick Miller of the Los Angeles *Herald-Examiner,* the official scorer for the game, had ruled that Miller made an error on the play. That took me off the hook. I still had the no-hitter going.

The Yankees were furious with the call. They all thought that Spencer should have been credited with a hit. They charged up onto the top step of their dugout and started waving at the press box, screaming out all kinds of stuff.

I found out later that there was a confrontation between our general manager, Buzzie Bavasi, and Dick Miller in the press box. Buzzie had promised a bonus of $25,000 to any Angel pitcher who threw a no-hitter.

"I'll give him $25,000 for a one-hitter," Buzzie screamed at Miller. "You didn't have to do that. You embarrassed us."

"The ball hit the tip of his glove" was Miller's answer. "I think he should have made the play."

When all the commotion settled down, I went back to work, but some of my concentration was broken. That controversy was an upsetting thing to go through. It was definitely a distraction. I didn't want a tainted no-hitter either.

I got the two remaining outs in the eighth and the game

moved into the ninth. Munson led off with a bouncer to short that Jim Anderson muffed. Again "E" flashed on the scoreboard. I still had the no-hitter. I got Nettles on a little pop-up. That brought up Reggie Jackson.

He laid his bat on my first pitch and slapped the ball past my glove up the middle into center field. It was a clean hit and broke up the no-hitter.

Reggie went up the line toward first base just a couple of steps, stopped, and turned. Then he waved sarcastically up at the press box.

Then when he got to first base he started applauding along with the crowd that was giving me a long standing ovation. That moment moved me. I realized I had lost the no-hitter, but also realized that it probably worked out for the best. I wouldn't have wanted to throw a no-hitter and have it constantly argued that it was a no-hitter only because of the official scorer.

The game finally came to an end when I struck out Chris Chambliss. The win brought my record to 12–6, and I wound up with the seventh one-hitter of my career to that point. It was a tough game, an exciting game, and a game that, I guess, Reggie Jackson and Rick Miller and Dick Miller and I will never forget.

Playing on the Angels never brought me that much national recognition. We were just another American League ball club. For some reason that game, maybe because it was against the New York Yankees, on national TV, brought me a lot of national recognition. And with all the talk of my becoming a free agent, it kind of showcased what people were calling the drawing power of a power pitcher.

The longer the 1979 season went on, the more I anticipated leaving Anaheim.

That's the way things were starting to fall. During the course of that season, Dick Moss stopped by Buzzie Bavasi's office. They got to talking and Buzzie said, "Just write out what it will take to sign Nolan Ryan today."

Dick and I really never talked about figures. But at that point Dick wrote on a piece of paper the figures of a million dollars for the first two years and $700,000 for the final year of a three-year contract. He passed the slip of paper to Buzzie, Dick said, and Buzzie was like to have a coronary.

Just after that, Buzzie put the word out that I was asking for a million dollars a year. He also started putting the rap on me in the newspapers. Within a week's time Buzzie had made such a big deal of it all that I became determined that as long as Buzzie was with California there was no way I was going to come back to the Angels for the 1980 season.

We put our Villa Park house on the market, packed all our belongings, had a moving van come in, and moved everything back to Alvin. I knew I was through with the Angels.

It was with quite a few regrets that I left California. I really liked the fans at Anaheim and had a special relationship with them. I felt I was appreciated by them as a person and as a performer on the baseball field.

I couldn't say the same things, however, about Buzzie Bavasi, a standoffish type of general manager from the old school. When it became clear that I would be leaving the Angels, he made the statement that all he had to do to replace me was to go out and find two pitchers with 7–6 records.

One of my biggest disappointments in the whole situation was Jim Fregosi. I thought he was going to be more supportive of retaining me as an Angel, since he had indicated to me that he planned on doing everything he could to keep me playing at Anaheim. I thought Jim should have gone to bat with Gene Autry. Since I was valuable to the club, it would have been in Jim's best interests to see that I was retained.

Maybe Jim became a little too comfortable after we won the division title in 1979. Maybe that changed his attitude into one of not taking sides. But I think Jim came to regret the way he acted because in 1980—when I was gone—California had a rough year, and he was fired.

Winning the division title in 1979 was satisfying, but it wasn't a sudden thing. In 1978 we had won eighty-seven games and finished five games behind Kansas City, in second place. So you knew the team was coming on. But I was really pleased that we won a division title for Gene Autry before I left the Angels. I probably was moved the most by what we had accomplished, since I was the elder statesman on the team, the one with all that longevity. Leaving Gene Autry and leaving the fans who had been so loyal to me was a moving experience. I appreciated those Angel fans a lot and wrote a thank-you letter to them and ran it in the Orange County *Register.*

The move back to Alvin was not disruptive to our kids. The two little ones, Reese and Wendy, were toddlers; they didn't know any different. Reid was aware of our baseball routine, moving around a lot. We would start him in school in California. When we moved back home in the fall, he'd go to school in Texas. And in the spring he'd go back to school in Anaheim.

For Ruth and me, though, it was the most draining kind of year, what with all the anxiety over Reid's accident, getting in the play-offs against Baltimore and not winning, the free agent deal hanging over our heads constantly, and the verbal battles waged with Buzzie Bavasi in the press over my free agency.

Going into the free agent reentry draft, I thought that I could get a salary of $600,000 a year. Dick Moss thought we could do even better than that.

More than a dozen clubs drafted me, including Houston (which had been purchased by John McMullen during the 1979 season), Texas, Milwaukee, and the New York Yankees.

After the draft was over, George Steinbrenner, the Yankee owner, asked Dick Moss, "What's it going to take to sign Nolan Ryan?"

"One million dollars a year," was Dick's answer.

"It's worth it," Steinbrenner said. "Nolan's one of the most desirable quantities in baseball," he told reporters. "He's a strikeout king, and in these days when you have to fight soccer in the summer and football in September, you have to get the fans to the ballpark, somehow. And they come to see players hit home runs and strike people out."

Dick Moss called to give me the news. "I already have received a million-dollar offer from George Steinbrenner," he said. "Nolan, if I had your talent and charisma and could create the kind of excitement you can, I would want to do my thing in New York City because I think it's the greatest baseball city in the country. Just tell me if you want to become a New York Yankee."

"I don't want to become a Yankee," I told him. "I don't want to go back to New York City. I've been through that all before."

"All right, Nolan," Dick said. "You know your own mind, but we have the Yankee offer to fall back on if we want to."

In the middle of all of that, Bill Rigney, who had been the first manager in the history of the Angels and was a special-assignment person, telephoned me. Rigney wanted to know what it would take to get me to go back to the Angels.

"I'm not going back, Bill," I said. "I'm not going back as long as Buzzie is there with the team. There's been enough said and enough hard feelings. I don't want to play for the man or be associated with him."

The day after the draft, John McMullen visited with Dick Moss and told him that the Astros wanted to sign me. When Dick gave me the news, I instructed him to make every effort to get me signed with Houston because I didn't want to get into a bidding war with those other teams.

The Astros were the only ball club we ever negotiated with, and although a lot of people said I participated in free agency to play for Houston, I never expected to sign up with that franchise. Houston had never taken part in the free agent draft before. So it was just a bonus for me to return home.

I never got in a position where I had to choose between signing up with New York or Milwaukee or Houston. That was never an issue. We didn't negotiate with other ball clubs, so we don't know what our maximum figure would have been. We negotiated with one ball club—Houston. Steinbrenner's offer of $1 million was a floor, but we didn't build off of that. Basically, what Dick Moss did was to get Houston to match it.

I signed a three-year contract for $1 million a year.

Buzzie Bavasi had claimed that I had asked for $1 million a year from the Angels. But the truth was that I had not asked for $1 million. I had asked for much less than that. If Buzzie had given me what I'd asked for, he would have had a bargain, and I'd probably still be pitching for the California Angels. What Buzzie did was make it possible for me to move on and make a lot more money. Later he admitted not signing me was one of the mistakes he made in his career.

PART IV

· · ·

HOUSTON

was looking forward to coming home and playing for Houston. It was a dream fulfilled. Just about a month after I signed with the Astros, there was a "Welcome Back to Texas Day" staged for me in Alvin. About two thousand people turned out. That's an awful lot of people for Alvin. Everyone had a festive time. The head of the Chamber of Commerce said, "We in Alvin are just dad-burned proud of you." I was dad-burned pleased to be back home in Texas, too.

After a while, though, a few problems developed over the fact that I was going to be paid $1 million a year. Nobody had ever been paid that much money in salary in any professional team sport before.

JIM WATSON:

We were pleased as punch to have Nolan back home. But among my cohorts in Alvin almost every day there were debates over his million-dollar contract. There were articles in the local paper, letters to the editor: "No baseball player is worth that kind of money. . . . Now Ryan doesn't have to work hard." That was the kind of stuff that was said and writ-

ten. Texans are proud people, and Nolan had the burden on
him to prove to them that he was worth it. I knew he was. I told
all of them, "You wait and see: Nolan is worth every penny that
McMullen will pay him."

RED MURFF:

Nolan's signing and coming home to Texas created a new
interest in the Houston franchise. It also made people get all
swept up in the controversy about the money he was going to
receive. "He deserves the money—he's not worth that kind of
money"—that kind of talk went back and forth at gas stations,
fraternal gatherings, barbershops, all over the place. It was
going on every day. Around the Houston area, Nolan Ryan's
big contract became almost as big a topic of conversation as
oil and cattle. For Texas, that was something else.

Some of the people in Alvin we had grown up with began
acting uncomfortable around Ruth and me. It was as if they
expected that we had changed because I was earning so
much money. Even my brother and sisters were a bit over-
whelmed by the contract I had signed. It seemed that people had trouble being relaxed in our company. The air and
the atmosphere and the comments that were made about
our being so rich—that kind of stuff really annoyed me.
Because we hadn't changed. We weren't about to change
our life-style. We didn't go out and buy a luxury boat or go
on a world cruise.

Time told the tale. People eventually realized that Ruth
and I weren't any different than we had been before the

contract was signed. It took a while, though, for them to realize this.

Lots of people came up to me with investment ideas and schemes. I'm so conservative and I mingle so little that I didn't get as many of those kinds of offers as others in my situation might have. But still I got some.

I got letters from people from all over inquiring what I planned to do with all my money. None of these people claimed to be long-lost relatives. Yet they could have been members of the family what with all the interest they were showing in me.

One guy wrote to me taking exception to the size of my million-dollar contract and also claiming I had totally sold out by posing as the cowboy in the Marlboro cigarette ad.

"Don't you know that cigarettes cause cancer," the guy wrote, "and you're supposed to be a clean-living model for the youth of America?"

I wrote back to him that I wasn't the one posing for the ad. But he didn't believe me. He mailed me a copy of the ad and a picture of myself. "Anybody can see," he wrote, "that you and the cowboy are one and the same. You can't fool the public."

I tried to get by with the same approach I had used with success in the Nixon case: the autographed picture and the line about the great fan. That didn't do any good. The guy was irate and persistent. He kept on writing. Finally the letters stopped. That guy probably came up with some other topic and some other athlete to complain about.

Money poses problems for players. So many things are

taken care of for them in baseball that they're really not equipped to handle large amounts of money. I certainly wasn't prepared to handle the kind of money I was suddenly earning. I had no background in taxes or finances. Basically, I went out and invested my money in real estate and ranching and stuff to keep, not in speculative things. I upgraded my ranch in Gonzalez, outside of San Antonio, thinking in terms of what I planned to do with my life after baseball.

PHIL GARNER:

This is the day of the big-money guys, ballplayers driving Rolls-Royces, living in condos in Hawaii. Money may have changed them, but it didn't change Nolan Ryan. I remember a couple of years ago we stopped in a small country town during a hunting trip. Nolan needed some gun oil—that's stuff that you rub on your gun. In west Texas it gets dry and dusty, so you have to use gun oil. Nolan went into a little old country store, picked out a bottle of gun oil, and set it down on the counter. The little girl rang it up.

"Two dollars thirty-nine," she said.

"What?"

Nolan was kind of shocked. He took that gun oil off the counter and put it back on the shelf. The girl didn't know it was Mr. Ryan there with the gun oil. He was driving a pickup truck and was dressed in rough clothes just like everyone else in that little country town. But he wouldn't buy the gun oil because he knew it wasn't worth the price. It showed the guy still knows the value of a dollar and has values that he hasn't gotten away from.

The day of the signing I made a statement to the press: "In two or three years this contract will not seem so astronomical. It will be just another contract." And they thought I was crazy, but it's come to pass. I'm probably thirty-fifth to fiftieth in players' salaries now. There are almost sixty players earning more than a million a year. There are guys now earning almost double my salary.

Once I thought if I could ever make $100,000 a year in this game I'd have it made. I made that much my third year in Anaheim. It made me realize you never reach a level that solves all your problems and puts you in a position where you don't have to work. People would say, "Look at Nolan Ryan. Look what he makes. He's rich."

Well, you know, I don't view it that way. Money enables me to do things on just a larger scale than I normally would. But it also increases my obligations and responsibilities.

I owe a lot to baseball and feel very fortunate that I came along when I did. I could've come along twenty years earlier and not benefited as I have, but the other side of the coin is that I could have come along ten years later and might be making almost double what I'm making now.

I don't think John McMullen, the Astros' owner, ever anticipated the repercussions my signing that contract would have on his organization as far as its pay scale was concerned. My contract was the spur that eventually escalated everybody's salary.

J. R. Richard was the highest-paid player on the Astros till then, and he renegotiated his contract because of the money I was making. Then the ball club had two salary arbitration cases that involved Joaquin Andujar and Joe Sambito. Those players used the salary I was being paid in their arguments against the Astros, and they won. But all of that didn't keep McMullen from spending money. He went on to re-sign Joe Niekro to a large contract and paid Don Sutton a lot of money as a free agent to join the team in 1981.

There were pressure and distraction everywhere I went in 1980. Everybody wanted to talk about the money I was making. I felt pressure to perform and knew that a great deal was expected of me. I told people they shouldn't be influenced by the size of my contract and think that it was going to turn me into a twenty- or twenty-five-game winner. I told them to judge me by my track record because I felt capable of performing up to that.

One thing that helped me feel comfortable coming into that Houston situation was that Bill Virdon was there as the manager. He had managed me at Williamsport in 1966 and Jacksonville in 1967, so I knew what to expect. I liked him. Bill was an ex-marine, a stern person, but a fair person. He had a set of rules, and you always knew where you stood with him. His rules were not flexible. You could go in and discuss things with Bill. He might end up agreeing that he wasn't right about something, but he wouldn't change his decision.

Nowadays in baseball you almost have to be a manager of

personalities, you have to be understanding of people's needs and wants. I think managing is a lot tougher now than it was twenty or thirty years ago. Managers like Virdon would be too rigid for today's players, and I think Bill realized that when he finished up his managerial career with the Montreal Expos.

The players on the Astros were very warm to me, very pleasant. They all read the hype about my being brought to Houston to help them win a pennant and they all knew the details of my contract. Still they welcomed me. They were a good bunch of guys.

That 1980 team had Jose Cruz in left field, Cesar Cedeño in center, and Terry Puhl in right. Alan Ashby was the catcher. Art Howe played first base along with Denny Walling, and some third base. Enos Cabell was the regular third baseman. Craig Reynolds was the shortstop and Joe Morgan played second base. What's unusual about the Astro organization is that basically this club has been together longer than any other current team. The 1980 Phillies, for example, have only two guys left: Mike Schmidt and Greg Gross. Going into the 1987 season our team still had me, Puhl, Reynolds, Walling, Ashby, Cruz, Dave Smith—about seven or eight players. We've always had a good nucleus, a low-profile club with no big egos in the clubhouse bouncing off each other. That's why we've never had any controversy or fighting among the players.

J. R. Richard had been the National League strikeout leader with Houston in 1979, and I had led the American League in strikeouts. People had always gotten into comparing how fast we both were. Now we were thrown together, and I guess J.R. knew that he had to share the limelight with somebody else, whereas before he had been the big-name pitcher for Houston. J.R. didn't warm up to me as much as the other players did. Still, we got along, we even went fishing together during spring training.

In the middle of the season, in the midst of the pennant race, our Astro team lost J. R. Richard. He collapsed on July 30 during a workout in the Dome. He was rushed to the hospital and went through emergency surgery to remove a blood clot in his neck. The doctors said he had suffered a major stroke. J.R. was out for the rest of the year. He was never the same again and couldn't continue with his career. Richard had been our stopper up until then, but as things worked out he wasn't missed quite as much as we thought he would be. Vern Ruhle took J.R.'s spot in the rotation and had an outstanding second half of the season.

Coming to Houston, I linked up with catcher Alan Ashby, and I've thrown to him longer than anyone else in my career. It was no great transition working with Alan—I throw 70 percent fastballs and call my own game, so there were no problems. Ever since I've been with the Astros, they've tried to make Alan the second catcher. They're always bringing somebody else in, but Alan has endured through it all. Alan Ashby is a fine all-around catcher, a player who has never fully gotten his due.

ALAN ASHBY:

> I don't use any more protection to catch Nolan than I do with anybody else, but that doesn't mean he doesn't punish me more than the others. I've got a forefinger that has been under doctor's care. I've lost circulation in it, and probably Nolan more than anybody else is the one I should blame for that. He likes to complain that I wear a pad under my glove and that my glove doesn't pop that much and his fastball doesn't sound like a great fastball to all the fans. He doesn't only want to look good on the mound—he wants to sound good, too.
>
> Nolan always has the final say on pitches he wants to throw —he never throws a pitch he doesn't want to unless it's one a batter hits out of the park. Then it was my pitch.
>
> But seriously, Nolan's the greatest power pitcher the game has ever known. You find yourself almost in awe of the guy when you play with him.

The 1980 season was a long one for me. I began with my usual slow start in spring training. If I ever had to make a ball club on the basis of my spring training performances, I'd never succeed. Then once the 1980 season was under way, we were in a pennant race the whole time with the Dodgers.

On the Fourth of July I recorded my 3,000th career strikeout, getting Cesar Geronimo of the Cincinnati Reds. Cesar was also the 3,000th strikeout of Bob Gibson's career. Afterward they asked him how he felt about going into the record books with Gibson and me. "I just happened," Cesar said, "to be in the right place at the right time."

I felt I was in the right place at the right time pitching for Houston, living at home in Alvin, but I split my first ten decisions in 1980. Adjusting to a new league took some time.

I found they didn't call the high strike in the National League the way they did in the American League. I would say that, pitching again in the National League, I found the strike zone shrunk for me by about 25 percent. I also had to adjust to hitters who had different styles and personalities, batters like Dave Winfield and Mike Schmidt.

DAVE WINFIELD:

I had a perception of Nolan Ryan when I was in college. He was a guy that threw scary fast. When I batted against him I knew he had the potential to throw a no-hitter every time out. With us, people saw a classic duel—power versus power. He's coming with that mighty fastball. I'm a big target and he doesn't have to be that fine with me. The question is can I get around on him.

I remember a game in 1980, which was my final season in the National League with San Diego and Ryan's first season with Houston. The game plan for pitchers seems to have always been to bust me in with fastballs, to curve me away. I don't know what was on Ryan's mind that day—we never said two words to each other. But he buzzed three pitches pretty close to me. The third time his fastball was really up and in. I was livid.

I started out to the mound to get him. "Dammit," I yelled, "don't you ever throw at me." He didn't say anything. I charged him, but he just stood there on the mound. I swung at him, but he ducked. Then we did some grappling out there on the mound and were swallowed up by bodies from both teams. He stayed in the game and I was thrown out. A few years later in the All-Star Game in Minnesota I faced him again. And he knocked me down again.

I don't know why Winfield got so fired up except that maybe it was because he was playing out his free agency year. I know how that can take its toll. But I've thrown a lot of pitches closer to many others than I threw to him. Satchel Paige used to call that kind of pitch "the old bow tie."

With Mike Schmidt I learned that the best approach was to put him in the hole, get ahead in the count and make him aware of my curveball. If I'm ahead in the count my fastball doesn't have to be that fine. What people don't realize about a power hitter of Mike Schmidt's caliber is that he is so disciplined at the plate. The tough thing about him is that if you don't give him a good pitch to hit he'll take it and wait for another one. He'll take a base on balls. He won't swing at bad pitches unless he's fooled. I respect Mike a lot.

GERRY DAVIS:

I've been a National League umpire for a while now. One of the things I look forward to is a Mike Schmidt–Nolan Ryan confrontation. When they go at each other, Ryan takes a little more time between pitches, but not too much time. He doesn't want to irritate a batter like Mike. Schmidt will sometimes step out between pitches, but not too long. He doesn't want to show up Ryan.

MIKE SCHMIDT:

With Nolan Ryan, I've always had to step up my game a notch. For the normal major league pitcher, you sometimes may have the freedom to concentrate on something other than the ball. I may be able to think of where my hands are or where my feet are. With Nolan, I've got to go up into the batter's box and get low, get solid, and say, "All right, baby, it's me and you. My swing and your fastball."

Since we began facing each other, our competition was the thing to watch. Nobody gets up and goes for a beer in Philadelphia when I'm hitting against Nolan Ryan. Nobody in Houston goes for a beer when he's pitching against me. Those are the confrontations that make baseball the great game that it is.

Obviously, Nolan has gotten the upper hand on me over the years. I have beat him with home runs a few times. I would like to have had more hits against him, just as a thousand other major league hitters would like to have done. But there are very few hitters, right-handed hitters anyway, who wear him out.

He's always had the great curveball, and now he's got a great change-up to go along with it. He's always been tough for me to hit. He used to throw me off balance and fool me with his curveball. Now he's got another pitch to fool me with.

I don't believe we've said ten words to each other through

the years in direct conversation. We exchange hellos, how ya doings, and maybe a little kidding line here and there. Our paths haven't crossed. He's not a golfer. We're not from anywhere near each other.

I'm as close to retirement as he is, and it's at bats against N.R. that make me say, "Gee, I can't wait till it's over so I don't have to go through this anymore."

You think it'd be fun, a challenge, but when a guy throws a 95 mph fastball and a hook that drops off the table, the odds of your getting a hit are very low. You go up there every time thinking that you're going to get a line drive somewhere. In essence, it takes a real good game out of you as a hitter to hit Nolan Ryan's pitches.

The way to beat him is to get eight hitters working deep counts, a couple of walks, a couple of stolen bases, a hit-and-run, maybe somebody hits a home run. You have to do it in an inning. You're not going to hit him around every inning. There may be, in a seven- or eight-inning stint by him, a couple of innings that you get base runners. You have to take advantage of it. That's how you're gonna beat Nolan Ryan, because he's going to blow you away three quarters of the innings he pitches.

He's special . . . really special. My friend and I—another guy on the club—imitate him all the time. We play catch and pretend we're Nolan Ryan. Say all you want about Mike Scott, when the Astros come to town you worry about facing Nolan Ryan.

What kept the Astros leading in the 1980 National League West race against the Dodgers was our relief pitching. In five weeks between July 1 and August 17 our starters were able to complete only six games.

On August 24 Bill Virdon announced, "I'm giving Ryan the ball tonight, and unless he gets hurt, he's going nine innings."

When I arrived at the Dome, there was a note tacked up over my locker: "Go nine." And it was signed "The Bullpen."

I had heard what Virdon had said and knew the bullpen was dead tired and that its sign was for real, so I went out and pitched a nine-inning two-hitter against the Chicago Cubs to give our team its tenth straight win.

Back spasms affected me from time to time after that win for the rest of the season, but our team continued in the dogfight with the Dodgers. With three games remaining in the season, we had a three-game lead over L.A. If they swept us, there would be a one-game play-off.

I learned later that there was a sign on the door of the Dodger clubhouse: "Anyone who doesn't think we can win four in a row—don't bother to get dressed."

They all got dressed and they almost swept us. They won the final three games of the season. Fortunately for us, Joe Niekro pitched a gutsy six-hitter in the one-game play-off, and we beat the Dodgers, 7–1, to win the National League West.

The championship series against the Phillies was very exciting but kind of anticlimactic. We split the first two games with them in Philadelphia and then went back to Houston.

Pete Rose, then with the Phillies, was always the first guy from the visiting team on the field, and he was always talking to everybody. Pete couldn't hit a good fastball in on him when he was batting left-handed. But he could foul it off. He'd keep battling you, waste your pitches until you gave him a better or a different kind of pitch to hit. And he was always a good breaking-ball hitter. In 1980 every time I faced Pete and had him set up for the curveball, somehow I'd always miss. I just could never get that breaking ball over to him for a strike.

"Nolan." Pete walked over to me in the Dome before the fourth play-off game. "How you doing?" Then he went into some small talk. Finally he said, "I wish you'd throw your curveball for a strike just once."

"Why's that?" I asked Pete.

"Because I'll hit the damn ball off your blanking forehead."

I told myself, We'll just see about that.

In the fifth game of the play-offs, the second time I faced Pete, I had him all set up for the breaking ball. Then I threw probably as good a curveball as I threw all day.

Pete hit a line drive. It was a shot right back at me that would have hit me square in the face if I hadn't caught it. The whole time Pete ran out the play to first base he was grinning and pointing at me.

We came close to beating Pete Rose and Mike Schmidt and the rest of the Phillies and getting into the World Series, but not close enough. We lost the fourth and fifth games of the play-offs to Philadelphia in the tenth inning.

By the time that season was over, all the guys on the Astros were absolutely exhausted, mentally, physically, and emotionally. We were just glad that year of 1980 was behind us.

In 1981 a lot was being made of the fact that Pete Rose was closing in on Stan Musial's all-time National League record for base hits. When the season began, Pete was asked when he thought he might have a chance to break the Musial record. "Probably such and such a night in Philadelphia," he said, "and against Nolan Ryan."

That's how hooked Pete is on baseball and statistics. He was able to calculate to the exact time when he would have a chance to break that record.

In June we were in Philadelphia playing the Phillies. Pete Rose needed just two hits to break Stan Musial's record. In the first inning he slapped a single to right field off me.

I made up my mind that was all Pete was going to get off me. I was determined that I wouldn't be the one going into the record books with Pete Rose on that occasion. That was one spot in the record books I definitely did not want.

One of the beautiful things about baseball is that every once in a while you come into a situation where you want to, and where you have to, reach down and prove something.

Pete Rose came up and faced me three more times in that game. And each time he came up I struck him out. I believe it was the first time that Pete ever struck out three times in a game.

PETE ROSE:

You could see the way Nolan got up for it. Most of the pitches I saw. Some of those pitches, though, I only heard.

ALAN ASHBY:

You hear stories about a Denny McLain possibly tossing one up in the middle of the strike zone for Mickey Mantle to hit a home run at the end of his career. Maybe there are some players who want to get their names into the record book in that kind of vicarious way. Not Nolan. The last thing Nolan wanted was to have his name associated with Pete Rose's record.

LARRY DIERKER:

Nolan Ryan versus Pete Rose is the best one-on-one confrontation I've seen in all my years of broadcasting for the Astros. Man oh man—were they going at it. After the last strikeout, Rose slammed his bat down on his way back to the dugout. That's not characteristic of Pete. But after he got back into the dugout, he tipped his cap to Nolan.

I guess I really frustrated Pete because he wanted that record badly in that game. As it turned out, he had to sit around and wait about six weeks to get that hit.

The players' strike began on June 12, 1981. A lot of fans were turned off by all the hostilities between the owners and the players. It was a greater hardship on the players.

The owners had taken out strike insurance with Lloyd's of London. I wished I had done something like that. Since I was making more money than any other player in baseball, I lost more money—approximately 30 percent of my income. When you're making a million dollars a year, that's a lot of money to lose.

I had planned out the spending of that money. I had obligated myself to investments in more land for my ranch in Gonzalez. I had obligations to pay for cattle and feed and other ranching items. The loss of income as a result of the strike really screwed things up for me and created a cash flow problem that took a while for me to get over. Had I not been earning so much money, I would not have had such problems. So, in a way, they were good problems. Still, they were problems.

Nevertheless, I was very supportive of the Players Association. I felt I had benefited greatly from all the advances it had achieved from the time I had first come up to the big leagues. Back in 1966 the minimum salary was $7,000 a year, meal money was $7 a day, the highest salary any player earned was about $115,000 a year. Great strides had been made since then, and without the Players Association they would not have been possible. So although I lost more money in the strike than any other player, I realized I would never have been in the position to lose that money if it had not been for the effort of the association and the players who went before me.

I never anticipated the strike going on as long as it did. After it had lasted for about a month, most players scattered all over the place to wait it out or to get on with other things in their lives. Feeling that we stood a chance of losing the whole season, I became depressed over the lack of progress toward a settlement. I didn't want to talk about the strike or read about it in the newspapers or watch the news on TV. I was sick of it.

Finally I went about my business as if it were the off-season. Like a lot of other players, I quit working out. I also devoted myself full-time to activity on my ranch.

The strike of 1981 was finally settled after it had gone on for 52 days. A total of 713 games had been lost, as well as an estimated $100 million in player's salaries, tickets, and concession and broadcasting revenue.

The All-Star Game in Cleveland led off the second half of the 1981 season. Bob Knepper and I were picked as the All-Star team representatives for Houston.

We came into the clubhouse in Cleveland. Steve Carlton and Dick Ruthven were there representing the Phillies, along with Mike Schmidt and Pete Rose.

"Hey, hey, Pete," Schmidt shouted when he saw me, "look who's here—your old buddy Nolan Ryan."

Rose hadn't seen me since that night in Philadelphia when I struck him out three times. He turned around slowly from his stool in front of his locker. He looked at me. And then he shot me the finger.

MIKE SCHMIDT:

That was clubhouse humor. Pete Rose has more respect for Ryan than Nolan can imagine. I'm sure the feeling is mutual.

> They're two baseball pros. . . . Nobody can understand what went into a confrontation between Pete Rose and Nolan Ryan. I've seen Pete kiddingly taunt Nolan, "Give me that old curveball . . . get that heater up here, now." I'd never say anything like that to Nolan. I wouldn't want that added pressure on my hitting.

When the season started again, the people in charge worked out a deal that guaranteed a play-off spot to the team that was leading the division at the time of the strike against the team that won its division the second half of the season. That arrangement didn't make some teams too happy, but we on the Astros knew we would be getting a new life—if we could win the division in the second half of '81.

That '81 season was Fernando Valenzuela's rookie year with L.A. He was pudgy and he didn't look like much of an athlete and he couldn't speak English, but darn, he could pitch. Five of his first eight starts that year were shutouts, and he was the guy that made the Dodgers the team to beat as we battled them day after day for the second-half pennant of '81.

On September 25 they came in to play a series at the Dome. I was scheduled to pitch the Saturday game on September 26. Since it was a game of a lot of consequence in the heat of a pennant race, it was on national TV. Ruth, my mother, and other members of my family and friends were in the stands.

RED MURFF:

> I went to the game that day with my wife, and the gods looked down on us. I had my program with me. As the good scout, I always had my program with me. I wrote in it: "Control of curveball today." That was the only thing I wrote in it. Then I settled back and watched the zeroes on the scoreboard.

JIM WATSON:

> For some reason I didn't ask for tickets for that game. I made up my mind at the last minute that I was going, so I sat in the bleachers with the regular fans. We got to talking as the game moved along. The people there found out that I had been Nolan's high school baseball coach. So they took to cheering, inning after inning: "C'mon, Nolan, C'mon, Jim!"

I struggled early, walking three batters in the first three innings, getting behind in the count a lot. My fastball at the start was just average, but I knew I had a real good curveball that day. And I was throwing it for strikes.

Twice before that season I had gone into the seventh inning with a no-hitter in progress only to lose it. My last no-hitter had been in 1975, when I was twenty-eight years old. Now I was thirty-four, and I was beginning to think that maybe I didn't have the stamina to get the fifth no-hitter.

In the seventh inning I fell behind in the count to Dodger catcher Mike Scioscia. He sat on my fastball and hit it well to the alley in right center field. Terry Puhl had a long way to go but caught up to Scioscia's shot and made the catch. When that happened, I felt that I had a legitimate chance at that fifth no-hitter because in a no-hitter there's always one or two key plays, and if they're made they make the difference.

RED MURFF:

> Along around the seventh inning, when it became evident after Terry Puhl's catch that Nolan stood a very good chance to pitch the no-hitter, people in the stands starting counting down the outs. "Nine, eight . . ."
>
> A few rows in front of me a little baby started to cry and the mother and the father got into an argument. "We'll have to go home," the woman said.
>
> "Are you crazy?" The husband was beside himself. "Here's Nolan Ryan pitching a no-hitter and you want to go home. We're staying—this is history happening right now." They stayed, and the baby slept right through it all.

Going into the ninth inning, I had retired sixteen straight batters and given up no hits in the game. But each time I returned to our dugout no one mentioned the no-hitter. That old baseball superstition about not jinxing the pitcher who has a no-hitter in progress is a mighty respected custom.

Reggie Smith came up off the Dodger bench to pinch-hit. I had been facing Reggie for years and knew he would be looking for one thing: a fastball. I wasn't going to take a chance of hanging a curveball. I made up my mind to go right at him. If he was going to beat me, it was going to be against my fastball. I got him on three fastballs. Two outs to go!

Then left-handed-hitting Ken Landreaux came up. He was a tough out and didn't strike out a lot. I got him to do what I wanted: ground out. With one out left to them, Dusty Baker came up. He was batting .322.

DAVEY LOPES:

Nolan had a hell of a curve and a great fastball that day. All of us on the Dodgers appreciated his effort, but we all wanted to ruin his no-hitter. However, we just couldn't. Dusty Baker was all excited in the dugout. "Don't worry about nothing," he was screaming, anxious to get up there. "I'll get a hit. Don't worry about nothing. I'm gonna bust up that guy" (but the word he used wasn't "guy").

The count on Baker was 2–2. I looked into the on-deck circle and Steve Garvey was kneeling there. Of all the hitters in their lineup, the one I was most uncomfortable with was Garvey. He had a small strike zone and always had good swings off me. He was a tough out. The one guy I didn't want to face in that situation, pitching out of the stretch, was Garvey.

I had a feeling that Baker, a fastball hitter, was looking for my curveball. I also felt that even if he was looking for it he couldn't hit it.

I threw the curve. Baker hit the ball down to third base. Art Howe had it, and I knew I had the record-setting fifth no-hitter. We beat the Dodgers, 5–0, and that win put us right there in the pennant race.

I wound up with 11 strikeouts, the 135th time in my career that I struck out 10 or more batters in a game. I was excited that I was able to pitch that record-breaking fifth no-hitter. It was what I had wanted ever since I had gotten the fourth.

We all have childhood dreams and fantasies—and I always wanted to be an Astro. When I pitched for the Angels, because of the time difference in California my Texas friends and acquaintances hardly ever got the opportunity to see me. My accomplishments in the main were something they read about in the paper. To pitch that fifth no-hitter at home truly fulfilled my dreams and yearnings.

JIM WATSON:

When the ninth inning began, I started to make my way out of the bleachers and down to the barrier. I wanted to get over to Nolan and congratulate him. But there was such a crush of people that I managed to get only as far as the seats behind the Astro dugout. The guards stopped me there. I couldn't get out onto the field, so I just watched. Ruth was out there with the kids with Nolan and his mother and his in-laws. It was something special to see the greatest pitcher on top of the mountain. He wasn't doing cartwheels. He was there very happy, but calm and collected. And in control, the way he always is.

My teammates carried me off the field and were genuinely excited about the no-hitter, and that meant a lot to me. I was a guy who had come to Houston with a lot of publicity and with a big contract and they accepted me. Those guys from that Astros team are probably as good a group of people as I've ever played with.

The first phone call I received after I finally got into the clubhouse was from Gene Autry. He had watched the game on TV in California and he congratulated me. That's why my relationship with Gene has always been special. Even after I left the Angels he was never bitter toward me, didn't resent what I had done.

I received a lot of other phone calls and telegrams, and I even heard from Richard Nixon, who always seems to touch base with me when something special happens in my career.

RED MURFF:

I knew Nolan would be busy and I waited until about a week after that game to call and congratulate him on what he had done, something that no one in history had ever done—pitch that fifth no-hitter. He became the talk of the area—and no one was saying anymore that he didn't deserve that big contract. Texans, you know, are a funny kind of people. They like to brag and exaggerate. There were probably about forty thousand or so at the Dome when he pitched that fifth no-hitter. But I'll bet there are about a million people today who will say they were there.

My won and lost record for 1981 was 11–5, making it the first time since 1974 and only the second time in my major league career that I had finished six games over .500. I posted a 1.69 ERA to lead the National League. I had a great season.

The Astros won the "second half" pennant with a 33–20 record, and a lot of credit for that goes to our diversified pitching staff: Joe Niekro throwing the knuckleball, Don Sutton doing his thing, Bob Knepper, the left-hander, finishing second in the league in ERA.

BOB KNEPPER:

> Nolan's modes are different from mine, different from most pitchers'. His thinking is entirely different but it works for him. He just comes at you. I give him credit. You can't imagine how determined you have to be to throw your hardest fastball every time. It takes incredible concentration.

The Dodgers, who won the "first half" pennant, were our competition in the best-of-five series for the National League West championship. The Cincinnati Reds, who had the best won and lost record that season in the National League, didn't even get into the play-offs. They weren't too pleased with that, but the strike had created the new format and screwed things up.

I started in the first game of the play-offs at the Dome aganst Fernando Valenzuela. And we were both on our game. Through 8 innings we had both given up just one run. The Dodgers had scored when Steve Garvey homered off me. As I said, I never did like facing Steve, who had that small strike zone and compact swing.

In the bottom of the ninth inning Alan Ashby hit a two-run home run off L.A. relief pitcher Dave Stewart and we won the game, 3–1. I struck out seven in that game and gave up just two hits.

We won the next game, and everybody on the Astros was in an up mood. All we needed was a win in one of the three games scheduled at Dodger Stadium and we would move into the National League Championship Series, but things didn't work out for us.

The Dodgers won the next two games. Then I took the mound against Jerry Reuss in the fifth and final game. I gave up only four hits in six innings but left the game after the sixth trailing 3–0. Shakey fielding did us in. The Dodgers wound up winning the game 4–0, and our season was over.

We were all disappointed that we had gone that far and lost, but it seemed that the Astros just had a mental block as far as the Dodgers were concerned. We all remembered too well 1980, when they swept the final series against us and forced the one game play-off. For some reason our team did not perform well at Dodger Stadium, did not match up well against L.A.

We were all relieved that the 1981 season was over. It was a trying and confusing year. What with the negative publicity baseball had received because of the strike, the resentment of fans, the split season, the double play-off alignment, the year had been mentally and emotionally draining.

I entered the 1982 season in third place on the all-time strikeout list with 3,249. Gaylord Perry was in second place with 3,336. The big number—3,508 strikeouts, the Walter Johnson record—was now an attainable goal. I knew I had a real good shot at it. All I had to do was keep on pitching and avoid having some kind of crippling injury.

The Astros didn't have too good a year in 1982. We finished in fifth place. Losing Joe Sambito in the middle of the season hurt us a lot. In a way, losing Joe was one of the biggest setbacks the Astros suffered in the 1980s. Joe was a tough relief pitcher, a stopper from the left side.

We also lost Bill Virdon, who was fired in the latter part of the season and replaced by Bob Lillis, who had been with the Houston organization since its start.

As a team we didn't have the hitting, and there were some people who thought the Houston players were too laid back. "They're just a nice bunch of guys," Phil Garner said. "The Astros not only help you up after you've stolen on them, but they dust you off, too."

Our pitching staff, though, did its part that year. Joe Niekro won 17 games and was among the leaders in ERA. Don Sutton, signed as a free agent in 1981, was 13–8. He seemed to enjoy playing for the Astros. "I like the life-style in Houston," Don said. "You can wear your jeans here without people thinking you're trying to be stylish." However, late in the season, Sutton was gone. My old buddy Harry Dalton acquired Don for Milwaukee in a trade that gave us Kevin Bass.

I did all right that '82 season, winning sixteen games, and pitching the eighth one-hitter and the eighteenth two-hitter of my career. What everyone was making a fuss over, though, when the season ended was how close I now was to breaking Walter Johnson's record. My 245 strikeouts in 1982 brought me to within 15 to break the record.

It was back in 1969, when I was with Tom Seaver on the New York Mets watching Jim Bunning strike out his 2,500th batter, that I first heard the name of Walter Johnson. Tom told me he was the guy who held the all-time strikeout record, but I had never checked out the man or his record.

I'm just not into records. Pete Rose takes record books and baseball books and reads them all the time. When Pete was closing in on Ty Cobb's hit record, he became a student of the man. He knew Ty Cobb inside and out.

I never got that involved with Walter Johnson. Still, closing in on his record, I became curious about the man. Going into the 1983 season, I purchased a baseball encyclopedia. I had never owned one before. I looked up Walter Johnson's record and saw that he died just about a month before I was born. I also saw that during his playing career he was about the same height and weight that I am.

I did some reading about him, too. Back in 1916 Ray Chapman, then an infielder with the Cleveland Indians, was hitting against Johnson. Chapman started heading back to the bench. The umpire told him, "You've got another strike coming."

"Keep it," said Chapman. "I don't want it."

Smokey Joe Wood, a pretty good fastball pitcher himself, said this about Walter Johnson: "He could throw the ball by you so fast you never knew whether you'd swung under it or over it."

I realized that Walter Johnson was truly deserving of his Hall of Fame recognition and that he was a true baseball immortal. By the time spring training of 1983 came around, I was like a racehorse all saddled up to run at that Walter Johnson record. But I had to hold back for a bit. First I missed a good deal of spring training because of some aches and pains and wound up getting in only eighteen innings of pitching. Then I was hospitalized with prostatitis. It wasn't until our twelfth game that I finally got my first start of the 1983 season.

That game was on April 17 against Montreal. I got seven strikeouts, including number 3,500—the hitter was Andre Dawson.

My next start was against the Phillies, and I now needed eight strikeouts to break Walter Johnson's record. Maybe I tried too hard. I struck out only three, walked six, and lost the game 6–3.

On April 27, 1983, I started against Montreal at Olympic Stadium in a day game before a crowd of 19,309. I needed just five strikeouts to break Walter Johnson's fifty-six-year-old record. The Montreal manager was Bill Virdon, so there was a touch of irony there. I wondered if he thought back to those long-ago days at Williamsport and Jacksonville.

In the second inning I got Tim Wallach and Tim Blackwell on strikes. Then a couple of innings later I got Bryan Little. I wanted to get the record in that game. I needed only two more strikeouts, and all the fuss would be over with.

In the eighth inning I struck out Tim Blackwell to tie the record. Then Virdon sent Brad Mills, a left-handed batter, up as a pinch hitter. I had faced Mills only once before in my career and he had singled off me. Now Mills was the only thing that stood between me and the Johnson record.

I walked around a bit on the mound, not wanting to rush my delivery. My first pitch to Mills was a fastball on the outside corner—strike one! My second pitch was a little low, a little outside. Mills couldn't hold up and swung right over it. Strike two!

I wasted a fastball outside. Alan Ashby then gave me the sign for the fastball again. I shook him off. I wanted to throw the curve. I threw what we call a back-door curve, which starts outside and breaks over the outside corner low and away. Mills took it. Umpire Bob Engel threw a hard jab into the air—strike three! Strikeout number 3,509! As Mills said later, "I was looking for a fastball, and he threw a curve and I got vapor-locked."

The fans at Olympic Stadium gave me a standing ovation, and I took my cap off to them. Then likenesses of Walter Johnson and me were illuminated on the electronic scoreboard. Alan Ashby and Phil Garner came over to shake my hand and congratulate me on getting the record.

LARRY DIERKER:

When Pete Rose broke Ty Cobb's record, the entire stadium was full and first base was just like an anthill. When Ryan broke Johnson's record, they saved the ball and made an announcement and he kept on pitching. It almost seemed fitting that it happened that way because it showed Nolan's low-key approach to his achievements.

It was a fine moment, but it was one that was expected. Once I got close, everyone knew that record was going to fall. I also knew that Steve Carlton was going to break the record and that Tom Seaver and Gaylord Perry also stood a realistic chance of doing it. But it was special to be the first to break a record that most people once thought was going to stand forever.

The Johnson record was as meaningful to me as the five no-hitters and the single-season strikeout record. I get satisfaction out of knowing I broke the record in less than 16 seasons and in 2,500 fewer innings than it took Johnson to set it.

There were all kinds of congratulations extended to me when I broke the Walter Johnson record. One of the disappointments about all that was that I never received congratulations from John McMullen, the owner of the Houston ball club. He wasn't there. The commissioner wasn't there, either. When you accomplish things like that the person you work for should at least acknowledge it.

When I broke Johnson's record, I set a goal to become the first one to get to 4,000, but I didn't think of that until I got close and realized it was attainable.

Are 5,000 strikeouts attainable? I wouldn't say that. If they are attainable, that number's two to three years away. But the odds on my achieving 5,000 strikeouts have to be a lot higher than on my achieving 4,000.

I'm mighty proud that I've struck out more batters than any other pitcher in the history of baseball. However, I've also walked more batters than any pitcher who ever played the game. That's a record I'm not proud 'of. My reputation for wildness has caused me quite a few problems, including the fact that I haven't gotten the close calls over the years. There's nothing I can do about that, although I have more control as a pitcher than most people think I do. I pitch for the corners on either side of the plate and usually can hit my spot.

DICK WILLIAMS:

When I was Nolan's manager with the California Angels, I had a deal with all the pitchers there. If they managed to throw any combination of eighteen ground balls or head-high line drives that were caught and they pitched the whole game and got the decision, I'd give them a brand-new suit of clothes.

Nolan said, "Well, I'm not that type of pitcher, but I'd like to get involved in that deal. Can you come up with some other kind of arrangement for me?"

"I'll tell you what I'll do," I said to Nolan. "You give me a game where you don't walk a man, and even if you don't go the full game but you get a victory—the suit's yours."

Well, Nolan was never able to do it. He tried his best, gave it all he had, but he always walked one or two, maybe five or eight. But he always also struck out more than he walked, that was for sure.

In 1983 I was managing San Diego and he was with Houston. Nolan pitched a complete game against us. He didn't walk anyone and he got the win.

I wouldn't give him a suit of clothes 'cause he was on the opposition. But the next day I had a fully chilled magnum of Dom Pérignon placed in his locker.

Every blue moon, I guess, something unusual takes place. There must have been a blue moon for that game I pitched against Dick Williams and his Padres, because in 1983 I led the league in bases on balls for the eighth time in my career and was running on a pace of about two strikeouts to every walk. That year I also posted a 14–9 record and one of the better earned run averages in the league. The Astros finished in third place in the N.L. West, four games ahead of Dick Williams's Padres.

One of the bright spots for us in 1983 was our shortstop, Dickie Thon. He led the league in assists at his position and in game-winning RBI's, and he hit twenty home runs. Defensively Dickie was not as good as Ozzie Smith, but offensively Dickie was much better. In my judgment, at that time Dickie was the best all-around shortstop in the National League.

On April 8, 1984, we were playing a game against the New York Mets at the Dome. Mike Torrez hit Dickie with a pitch just above and to the left of his left eye. The ball struck right between Dickie's eye and ear. It was frightening. Dickie hit the ground in a lot of pain and had to be carried off the field on a stretcher.

I've seen several players hit in the head by a pitch and it's not a very pretty sight. Dickie, however, is the only one I ever saw who suffered lasting complications. He didn't play again all that season.

Dickie not only had a vision problem from that beaning, but also developed some mental fears. I threw batting practice to him a few times to try to help him readjust. It didn't help much. He was having a lot of trouble seeing the ball away from him.

What happened to Dickie once again showed me just how unpredictable life is. He was on top of the hill one day and then . . .

Everybody on the Astros felt bad about what happened, but there was nothing much any of us could do. I tried to help Dickie by getting him a job at Alvin Junior College as an assistant baseball coach while he enrolled for courses, but unfortunately that didn't work out for him.

Dickie played part of the 1985 and 1986 seasons but just couldn't handle things the way he had. Then in 1987 Dickie tried to come back again but just couldn't cope and decided to take the whole season off. His not being able to play has been tragic for him, and not having him has been a big loss for the Astros.

As a team the Astros have been plagued by some key losses of personnel—J. R. Richard, Joe Sambito, and Dickie Thon. Those things are all part of the bad breaks of the game, but in a way Houston has had more than its share of those bad breaks.

The 1984 and 1985 seasons were mediocre for me and the Astros. I was on the disabled list twice in '84 and was subpar in '85, trying to get things straightened out.

We tied for second place in '84 and tied for third place the next year. It was a very down time in Houston, what with the oil crisis, the poor economy there, and people staying away from the Dome. In 1985 we drew only 3,621 fans to a game against the Giants and only 2,600 for a game against Atlanta.

I did, however, have two highly satisfactory moments within the space of four days in 1985. That, I guess, is what anyone's career consists of—the bad times and the good times.

Danny Heep and I had become friends in the early eighties when we were teammates on the Houston Astros. But Danny was playing for the New York Mets when I faced him on July 11, 1985. And at that time I needed just one more strikeout to reach 4,000 for my career. Danny, a good fastball hitter, always had reasonable success batting against me. I knew that he certainly did not want to become strikeout number 4,000. Players never want that kind of reverse recognition, going into the record book that way.

The key to that at bat was that I was able to get ahead of Danny in the count. He fouled off the first pitch. Then he took a fastball low and away for strike two. I had him in the hole. My third pitch to Danny was a real good curveball. He swung and missed. I had wanted to be the first one to attain 4,000 strikeouts from the time I broke the Walter Johnson record, and it felt real good.

Five days later I was in Minnesota for the All-Star Game. When I arrived there I was told that Pete Rose and I would be throwing out the first ball. Pete had his 4,000 hits and I had the 4,000 strikeouts, and that was the way they chose to honor us. I did feel honored and was truly touched by that moment.

That All-Star gathering of 1985 was kind of a reunion of people whose careers had crossed mine through the years. Dick Williams was the National League manager and one of his coaches was Deacon Jones, who had coached when I played for the California Angels. Goose Gossage was there, and I remembered pitching against him when I was in the American League. I also faced Rickey Henderson and Dave Winfield of the New York Yankees and knocked both of them down on 0–2 pitches. Winfield told people that he was used to it. But Billy Martin, then the Yankee manager, was going around after the game blasting me and telling everyone that I was throwing at his ballplayers for no reason at all. That was the way Billy has always been to me. I just haven't paid any attention to that kind of behavior. I just go about my business.

That 1985 season I joined Cy Young, Jim Bunning, Gaylord Perry, and Ferguson Jenkins as the only pitcher to win over one hundred games in each league to that point in time.

When the 1986 season began, Hal Lanier came over from the Cardinals and replaced Bob Lillis as manager of the Astros. I place Bob in the same category as a manager as Dave Garcia and Norm Sherry. They were nice people, low-key, but not stern enough. It's unfortunate, but today's players have a tendency to take advantage of that type of manager.

Yogi Berra came in as a coach. Every walk of life has its characters, and Yogi is one of the true characters of baseball. The things he says make some people feel that Yogi is not very smart. But Yogi is very alert, a real student of the game, a master of his trade. He knows everything that's going on in baseball. If you talk to him about other things, however, he has no clue what's going on in the world.

For people like Yogi Berra and Jimmy Reese, baseball is their whole life. Going to the ballpark, being at the ballpark, being in uniform—that's what they want out of life.

There's been a lot of stories attributed to Yogi. I guess it all goes back to his childhood. Once someone reportedly asked him, "How do you like school?"

"Closed" was Yogi's answer.

When he was playing for the New York Yankees, he came home one night after a game. "How's everything?" he asked his wife, Carmen. "What did you do today?"

"I took the kids to see *Dr. Zhivago.*"

"Oh no, Carmen," Yogi said. "Don't tell me they're sick again!"

Another time he came into a clubhouse and announced, "I just saw a great movie on TV."

"What was it?" one of the players asked.

"The Great Escape, starring Steve McQueen," Yogi said. "He must have made it before he died."

Yogi is the first guy to get to the Dome every day. If we're playing a night game, he gets there about noon, makes his phone calls, and then takes a nap in the coaches' room. And when he wakes up, he's ready to go. I really like Yogi and I think it's too bad there aren't as many characters like him around baseball as there used to be.

Yogi attributed his success as a player to Bill Dickey, the old Hall of Fame Yankee catcher, who had served as Yogi's personal tutor. "Dickey learned me all his experience," Yogi said. The way I see it, Yogi is a big asset to Houston. Now he "learns all his experience" to the Astros.

I went into spring training in 1986 less than optimistic about our chances to be competitive as a team. The Astros had basically the same personnel they had during the two previous years when Bob Lillis was manager.

But Hal Lanier came in as a rookie manager, made some changes, put in his own rules, and had a Cinderella year.

There are a lot of things I like about Hal. He's a protégé of Whitey Herzog, an aggressive manager who is always into the game.

And we benefited from some players having career years in 1986. Nobody anticipated that Mike Scott would become Houston's first Cy Young Award winner and have the kind of year he had. Mike won 18 games, pitched a no-hitter, and led the league in strikeouts and earned run average. Nobody dreamed that Glenn Davis would hit 31 home runs and drive in 101 runs and wind up as runner-up to Mike Schmidt for the Most Valuable Player Award. Kevin Bass had a big year and batted over .300. Billy Hatcher, obtained in a trade with the Cubs, turned out to be a smart acquisition for us. He was just fine in center field and gave us speed in the leadoff spot in the batting order. Charlie Kerfeld was 11–2 and gave us all we needed in middle relief. Dave Smith, who I consider one of the most underrated relief pitchers in the game, picked up 33 saves. Everything broke right for us.

We went 49–25 after the All-Star break—the best record for that half of the season in all of baseball. Our 96–66 overall record was the best in Astro history. Our pitching staff had 1,160 strikeouts—the fourth-highest total in major league history.

My own season was eventful as usual. In spring training I developed an arm problem. When it first started, I thought the problem stemmed from adhesions that might have built up in my arm from my not throwing in the wintertime.

Then the season began, and, pitching in a four-day rotation, I got off to a rocky start. I was pitching in pain. I pitched despite the pain, thinking it would work its way out, but the pain didn't go away. I took a cortisone shot. I rested a lot, but the pain was still there. In the first two months of '86 my record was 3–6.

Dick Wagner had come over to Houston in September of 1985 from the Reds and replaced Al Rosen as general manager. Al was under constant pressure from our owner, John McMullen, who would telephone him anytime from six in the morning to midnight. Al was afraid to make any moves for the team, any trades. He was always looking over his shoulder for criticism. Now that Al is with the San Francisco Giants he's working in a different kind of atmosphere. He's had the opportunity to make a lot of moves to improve that team. That's one of the reasons they were able to win the National League Western Division title in 1987.

I'd heard many unfavorable stories about Dick Wagner from other ballplayers who were with Cincinnati. They complained about his dress code rules, his being against facial hair, his negative attitude toward signing free agents. Still, I wanted to give him the benefit of the doubt. I didn't want to be influenced by hearsay. When Wagner was appointed Houston's general manager, I went to the press conference to hear what he had to say. I wanted to start from square one with him. But Dick Wagner isn't an easy person to get to know or to get a reading on. And I've had my difficulties with him.

In June of 1986 the problem with my arm was still continuing. Dick thought that if I spent some time on the DL, that would help my arm. I wanted to do whatever would be best for me and the ball club, so I agreed with Wagner and went on the disabled list from June 2 to June 24.

When I came off the DL, the pain was still there. The doctors said I could continue to pitch in pain, that it wouldn't do any further damage to my arm. I figured I'd just pitch through it all. Discomfort wasn't a new experience for me, anyway.

One of my most memorable games of the season took place on July 22. I hooked up with Floyd Youmans of Montreal at the Dome in an old-fashioned pitching duel. Through nine innings I allowed one hit and no runs. I finally came out of the game after walking two batters in the tenth. At that point I had struck out fourteen. Glenn Davis led off the bottom of the tenth inning with a home run. We won the game 1–0. That was the kind of year the Astros had.

I could sympathize with Youmans, who gave up just three hits and lost a heartbreaker, but I had been there before myself—quite a few times before.

Then all of a sudden, in late July, Dick Wagner informed me that he'd decided to place me on the fifteen-day disabled list again. He made that decision without checking with me and getting my thoughts on whether I agreed with it or not.

I was disappointed that Dick didn't have more regard for my judgment and experience. I felt he was treating me like some young player, and I felt that I deserved to be given more respect.

I was also upset with him because I felt that being on the DL wasn't going to do a thing to improve the condition of my elbow. We'd clearly seen that the first time I went on the disabled list, when it did no good.

Wagner's position was that he wanted to give me some time off to rest so that the team would have me available to pitch down the stretch. I couldn't fault him for thinking that way. However, the problem I had with his thinking that way was that I knew how I felt, knew what it took for me to pitch, knew myself, knew that I wasn't going to put my own personal numbers ahead of those of the ball club.

All during that second stint on the DL, I was chafing at the bit to get back in there and pitch. There was a lot of excitement in Houston and a pennant to be won and I wanted to be part of it all.

I came off the DL August 12 and pitched the rest of that season in pain. But I was pleased that I helped the team in my last 10 starts, posting a 5–1 record and a 2.31 ERA.

On September 24 I pitched eight innings against the San Francisco Giants, struck out a dozen batters, and allowed just one single. We won the game, 6–0, and clinched a tie for the Western Division title. I won my last four decisions to wind up with 253 career wins, tying Carl Hubbell for 34th place on the all-time list and 6th place among active pitchers. My record for 1986 was 12–8, with 194 strikeouts in 178 innings.

The New York Mets were our competition in the National League Championship Series. When the 1986 season began, a lot of the experts had predicted that we would lose a hundred games. We won almost a hundred games and finished ten games ahead in our division. The Mets had busted up their division, winning it by 21½ games. We knew that they had a lot of power and experience, a lot of talent, but we also had confidence in ourselves and knew we had a lot of pitching to throw at them. Additionally, we had been hot down the stretch, winning 23 of 32 games from September 1 on.

There were some hard feelings between the Mets and the Astros. Nothing much was ever said on the field, but neither team had much fondness for the other. Part of our feeling stemmed from the Mets' complaining all through that season. They charged that Mike Scott was scuffing the baseball, doctoring it up to make his pitching more effective. Ray Knight even accused me of putting a foreign substance on the ball.

Their whining about Mike and their charges of his scuffing the ball led to a lot of his effectiveness against the Mets. They were so psyched out by him that it didn't matter what he threw. And to Mike's credit, he remained calm throughout all the uproar that '86 season.

"If the Mets think I'm throwing it, fine," he said. "If it has them thinking I have another pitch, fine. It's to my advantage to have them think I have another pitch."

To the best of my knowledge, Mike Scott does not scuff the ball. At least, he's never admitted to me or anyone else that he does. I've been accused of scuffing the ball, too;

basically, the entire Houston staff has been accused of throwing scuffballs.

I don't scuff the ball as a regular practice, but I have fooled around once in a while. Lots of baseballs that are hit on the ground get scuffed. If you get one of those baseballs and you grip it in the right place, you can make that ball sink and do all kinds of stuff.

One time, about three, four years ago, I was sitting down in the dugout, getting ready to pitch a game in the Dome.

The umpires were having their pregame meeting at home plate. A few minutes before, somebody had been honored and had thrown out the first ball. When that happens, a baseball is usually not left on the mound. The one that is used as the first ball is given away as a memento.

There I was, sitting in the dugout with a warm-up ball in my glove. Then I got a passing thought.

I took the warm-up ball and rubbed it on the concrete floor of the dugout. But that didn't deface the ball nearly enough for my purposes. So I took the ball over to the sharp edge of our dugout and starting scraping. I was able to rip the cover of the ball about an inch. When I walked out onto the mound to start pitching in the game, I had that ball in my hand.

My first pitch of the game sailed high about 15 to 18 inches. My catcher, Mark Bailey, never laid a glove on the ball. It hit the plate umpire, Frank Pulli. He called that pitch a ball. Then he bent down, picked up the ball, which had a one-inch gash on it, and gave me a look like "What the heck is going on here?" And then he threw the ball out of the game. I was lucky he didn't do the same thing to me, but I guess he realized it was a joke all the way around.

When I first came up to the major leagues, practically all the relief pitchers were throwing spitballs. Then a rule was put in that did not allow a pitcher to go to his mouth while he was on the dirt part of the mound. That rule was there to prevent the spitter. So guys did other things to doctor up the baseball. K-Y Jelly and Vaseline and stuff like that were brought in.

When I was pitching for the Mets, Don Drysdale was at the end of his career with the Dodgers. Once I came out to the mound and picked up the rosin bag that Drysdale had been using. That thing was just loaded with grease after he had gotten through wiping his hands on it. I knew that he had been going for any edge he could and was pitching a spitball or a greaser.

Pitchers back then would also put pine tar on their gloves. They would put that sticky stuff on their fingers to help them get a firmer grip on the ball, so they would be able to throw a better curve. The real good curveball pitchers did that a lot of the time.

From what I've heard and read, Whitey Ford fooled around with a baseball any way he could. But Don Sutton was the first person I ever knew who scuffed a baseball. Some years back I managed to hit a home run off Don. Since I haven't hit too many home runs during my career, I arranged to have the ball returned to me. And that thing was all scuffed up.

On occasion I've pitched from about six inches in front of

the rubber when I've needed the big strikeout. And I know I'm not the only one who's done that.

You just rock up, step in the hole, and you're half a dozen inches closer to the mound. Normally there's enough dirt and stuff on the mound late in the game to cover things up, but you have to work the area to dig a hole to get your foot in. I did that now and then when I was with California, but I don't do it anymore. The whole deal requires too much preparation. The mounds are also flatter now.

I guess you could consider pitching from in front of the rubber an illegal pitch. But the other side of that is that it's done in the spirit of competition.

RON LUCIANO:

About 40 percent of the pitchers in the major leagues cheat or look for some kind of an edge. They put grease on the ball. They pitch from in front of the rubber or off to the side. If Nolan's pitched from in front of the rubber, what difference does it make? It's like the first baseman cheating and coming off the bag early when a runner is out by three feet. Nolan's going to strike the batter out anyway. You could put Nolan on the grass behind the mound and he'd probably blow the ball by the batter.

Corked bats have also been part of baseball since it began. As long as wooden bats are used in the major leagues, players will be doing something to them. They accused Howard Johnson of the Mets of having a corked bat last year because he hit a lot of home runs. But to hit a home run you have to hit the ball on the good part of the bat, and you have to hit the ball hard, whether the bat is corked or not.

My attitude about corked bats is the same as it is about the scuffed ball, the spitball, the pine-tar ball, whatever. You still have to throw the ball over the plate, and you've still got to hit it. None of those so-called tricks of the trade make any difference if a player doesn't have the ability. None of those tricks makes a player an instant winner.

My attitude about cheating or trying to get an edge or whatever is that it's all just part of the game. It always has been and always will be.

The first game of the 1986 best-of-seven series for the National League pennant began at the Dome on October 8. It was Mike Scott against Dwight Gooden. And the Mets complained before, during, and after the game that Mike was doctoring up the baseball.

Mike was really up for the game and on his game. He struck out 14, and we wound up beating Gooden and the Mets, 1–0, on a second-inning home run by Glenn Davis.

I started in Game 2 against Bob Ojeda. Through the first three innings I was on my game, too. I gave up no hits, striking out five of the first nine batters I faced. But the Mets got to me in the fourth and fifth innings and we wound up losing the game, 5–1.

We split the next two games with them, and the fifth game of the National League play-offs was held at Shea

Stadium on October 14 before a sellout crowd. I was scheduled to pitch against Dwight Gooden in a game we really
needed to win.

Members of the New York media asked me if coming
back to Shea Stadium for such an important game had any
special meaning for me. It did bring back some fond memories of the 1969 World Series, of coming to the big leagues,
and so on. But when I looked over into that Met dugout, it
meant nothing to me. There was a whole different set of
faces and nobody in the organization remained from the
time when I played for New York except for Bud Harrelson. He was there in uniform as third base coach. Bud had
been there when I played for the Mets.

The negative feeling that existed between the two teams
created an atmosphere that made you a little more aggressive as a player. I'm always very aggressive when I pitch, so
I didn't need any extra motivation. When I'm out on the
mound I don't consider myself a very nice person. I almost
hate the players I'm pitching against. I get to feeling a lot of
hostility. Normally, I'm a very quiet and reserved person
with a peaceful outlook on things. But when I'm pitching
I'm anything but that.

That approach to pitching is something I've had to develop through time. I've seen Tom Seaver and others
laughing, joking around, when they pitched. I've never felt
secure enough to do that. For me, pitching is my business—
strictly business.

Since Dwight Gooden was pitching against me, some
people billed that game as "the new Nolan Ryan versus the

old Nolan Ryan." I'd heard that kind of talk before. But my mind was on the game. I knew it was going to be a tough one, a low-scoring game. Our history as a team against Gooden wasn't good. We hadn't scored that many runs against him.

Dwight Gooden and Darryl Strawberry, too, had their reputations precede them. New York City is notorious for that kind of thing. I had heard about Gooden and Strawberry before they ever arrived on the major league scene. They were heralded for their potential.

I think that created some of their problems. Strawberry was given a big contract with the Mets before he ever accomplished anything. That's another way baseball has changed. When I first came up you were paid toward the end of your career for what you had accomplished. Nowadays you get paid on your potential. It's all out of whack!

No doubt Dwight Gooden is deserving of all the recognition he has received, because he is an exceptional talent. He was instantly successful. Still, he had his problems. The key to Gooden's success his first two years in the National League was that he was getting his curveball and fastball over consistently. But in 1986 Dwight Gooden wasn't getting his curveball over as consistently, which made his fastball less effective.

I place Darryl Strawberry in a class with Reggie Jackson. If you make a mistake with Strawberry, he's going to hurt you. But you can get him out. I think he's becoming a better hitter. Yet what pace he's developing at is hard to say. Time will tell.

Going into that Game 5 against the Mets, I was aware that the Mets didn't have a lot of respect for me because I hadn't done that well against them in 1986. I had lost three of four starts to them that year. They were confident they could beat me after four or five innings, that they could get to me. Some of the Met players made a point of saying that in the newspapers.

Those kinds of statements gave me a little more incentive to pitch in that game—not that I really needed it, because I wanted to win that ball game as much as any one I've ever pitched.

That day I felt as if Houston's chances hinged more on my performance than anybody else's. Working in a game like that with my team's back against the wall, I get even more withdrawn, more homed in on my pitching than I normally do.

In the second inning, though, I got distracted for a moment. Maybe "agitated" is a better word. Umpire Fred Brocklander obviously blew a call on a double play at first base that cost us a run. What happened was that Kevin Bass was at third. Craig Reynolds hit a ground ball and definitely beat the throw to first base. The TV replay showed that was the case. If Reynolds had been ruled safe, there wouldn't have been a double play and Bass would've scored from third. That should have been a sign of what kind of day it was going to be.

In the fourth inning I was the runner at first base and a grounder was hit to shortstop. I knew I was going to be out at second on a play that wasn't even going to be close. So there was no reason for me to slide. I went into second base standing up and sprained my ankle.

When I went back into the dugout, I knew I was hurt. But I didn't know how severe the injury was. Then as the game went on, the pain became worse. I wound up with a fracture on my heel.

All season long I had felt pain in my elbow, and that was hurting again, too. But in a game of the magnitude of that fifth game you block things out. I'd pitched in a lot of pain all year long to get the opportunity to be in a game like that, and I wasn't about to let my ankle or foot or elbow problems keep me from performing.

We scored a run in the top of the fifth inning. In the bottom of that inning I had a 3–2 count on Darryl Strawberry. I wasn't going to walk him. I was going to make him hit the ball.

I wound up just trying to throw a strike. The ball was down. It wasn't a bad pitch. I would have preferred the pitch up on his hands and in. Strawberry swung and kind of golfed the ball.

When it left Strawberry's bat, I was just concerned about whether it was going to be fair or foul. I never thought the ball was going out. But Strawberry's so strong, he hit it well enough to hit it out before it hooked foul. The ball was a line-drive home run to right field—fair by inches, over the wall by inches.

The game moved on through the October afternoon, tied 1–1. I had a lot of velocity on my fastball, a good-breaking curve. I was in pain, but I paid it no heed. We were hitting Gooden, but the Mets made quite a few fine fielding plays to keep us from scoring.

I came out of the game after pitching nine innings, striking out a dozen batters, allowing just two hits and one run. We should have won that game, 2–1, in nine innings, and would have if not for that Brocklander call. But it was the Mets who won the game, 2–1, in the twelfth inning.

That game was a do-or-die situation for our ball club. I threw 145 pitches in that game, well past my pitch limit. Even though it was a do-or-die situation for the ball club, coming out of the game had no special meaning for me. I was physically tired, but I was not disappointed about coming out of the game. I had gone about as far as I could go.

HERB SCORE:

I've been a Nolan Ryan watcher for a long time. I don't know how much better a pitcher can be than Nolan has been. That fifth game against the New York Mets was like a command performance for him.

There have always been comparisons between Nolan and me. I threw hard but I don't know how hard. It's the old story. You don't hit off yourself. I feel rapport with him and all the effort he's expended as a fastball pitcher through the years. You don't find too many pitchers grunting the way Nolan does when he throws the ball.

Youngsters today say, "I have only so many pitches left in my arm and I have to save them." Then you look at Nolan Ryan pitching into his forties and still blazing the ball after all the pitches he's thrown. Nolan Ryan's the proof that what those youngsters say is not so.

After that fifth game ended, the mood in our clubhouse was down. Everybody was disheartened. But Houston's not the type of club that dies over a tough loss like that.

We knew we were going back to the Dome. We had Bob Knepper, a left-hander who had given the Mets trouble, for Game 6. And we had Mike Scott coming back for the seventh game. I felt that the Mets were totally psyched out by Mike and that we still stood a real good chance of pulling the thing out. But it wasn't to be. It was the Mets' year.

I watched the Angels in the American League play-offs and had hopes that there would be a California-Houston World Series. I would have liked to have seen the Angels win for Gene Autry. He's waited an awful long time. Still, the Angels and Astros got real close—as close as you can get without winning.

It was great to get back home to Alvin during the off-season after that hectic year of 1986. I was able to catch up on my chores around my ranch, relax, and rest.

Every little kid seems to fantasize about growing up to play in the big leagues. But I always wanted to be a rancher. I've gotten the best of both worlds. I keep heifers on the 82-acre farmhouse property where we live in Alvin. West of town, near Rosharon, I have commercial cattle on 3,000 acres of land that I lease. My real working property, though, is about fifty miles outside of San Antonio. On 2,000 acres there, I have 250 head of registered Beefmaster cattle. That breed is part Brahman, part Hereford, part shorthorn. Those Beefmasters originated in Texas more than fifty years ago.

I love being around cattle. And sometimes out on the range my mind drifts back to when I was twelve years old and to that first little calf I bought for $2.50 that I brought home in a feed bag.

Having what some folks would call my cowboy life to go back to when I'm not playing baseball is probably one of the things that accounts for my longevity. Working with cattle, hunting, fishing, being in the great Texas outdoors is a perfect release for me after the pressures of baseball season.

I think another reason I have lasted so long in baseball is my attitude toward the game. Pete Rose can come up to me and ask, "Last week when you gave up that home run to Mike Schmidt, what did he hit?" And I'm thinking, last week . . . home run . . . Mike Schmidt? Or Pete will say, "Ten days ago so-and-so went two for three against you. What did he hit?" Pete studies box scores and he remembers. Maybe that preoccupation works for him. As for me, when a game is over, it's over.

I can't remember the day after I've pitched how many batters I walked the night before. I don't recall two weeks after the season ends what my record is for sure. When the season is over, I absolutely put it out of my mind and start thinking of all the things backed up on me that have to be done.

I think that's one reason I've played as long as I have—I keep the game in its place. I never take the game home with me.

I've come across players who bust up things or sulk or take out their problems on those around them. I have never done anything like that. I have never taken out any of my baseball frustrations on my family.

It's very seldom that I read newspaper accounts of my pitching performance. I will look at the box scores to see how teams and players are doing, but I don't rush out and go out of my way to read what is written about me. But if I hear about something that's been reported about me that's inaccurate, then I'll call the writer up and try to get things straightened out.

So my attitude about the game has to help account for my longevity. Also, I believe I've lasted this long as a power pitcher because I'm a real strong believer in conditioning. I don't smoke or drink anything stronger than an occasional beer, and I watch what I eat, but most important, I'm dedicated to my conditioning program all year round.

PHIL GARNER:

Nolan has not lost his edge or his desire to train to perfect his game. And that's been the key to his longevity. Most guys get into their late thirties and they lose the will to get and stay in shape. God gave Nolan a great body and a great right arm. But he developed the attitude to keep it all going.

I have to give credit to Gene Coleman, a Ph.D., now at the University of Houston at Clear Lake. He used to work with the Astros in their training program and he designed a special conditioning program for me.

During the season I follow a very rigorous, very precise kind of program day after day. The only tricky element is that at my age I always have to listen to my body. If we come in from a road trip and I'm tired or if I'm a little under the weather, I back up my program a day or I modify it a bit.

Under normal conditions, the day after I have pitched I'll go into the weight room and do my lifting program. That procedure will take about an hour. Then I'll run about twenty wind sprints.

Back in my high school days Jim Watson ran us a lot. When I came to the big leagues they also made pitchers run a lot. Pitchers like Steve Carlton don't believe in the value of running. Although I'm certainly not one to criticize Steve Carlton and all the success he's had without running, I believe in running because I know that legs are very important to a pitcher's success. A lot of injuries also come when pitchers' legs get tired and they try to overcompensate by overthrowing with their arm. I believe that a good deal of my longevity has come from the power I've been able to generate with my legs.

Another part of my routine that helps my legs is riding the stationary bicycle for about twenty-five minutes. That is also very good cardiovascular exercise to get the heart rate up. I also do some dumbbell exercises to strengthen my shoulders and my arm. Finally, I also do different types of sit-up routines to strengthen my abdominal muscles. The whole program is strenuous and concentrated and lasts about two and a half hours.

LARRY DIERKER:

> I like to describe Nolan Ryan as a freak of nature. The raw ability has been given to him, but other players with similar ability never accomplished what he has. Nolan has an incredible work ethic. I work out with him on the weight machines and can do only about three quarters of what he accomplishes— and we're both the same age. I just get worn out and have to give up.

On the second day after I've pitched, I go back into my training routine with some modifications. I don't lift any weights. I throw for about fifteen minutes on the mound just to get loose and to get over any stiffness that I may have. I do the dumbbell exercises, ride the bike, and do the wind sprints again.

On the third day I repeat the exact program that I do on the first day. The fourth day is reserved for resting and for loosening up just a little bit. I do a lot of stretching, and that's an activity that keeps me limber and loose. And then I go out and pitch on the fifth day.

Aside from the elbow surgery I had in 1975, I've never had any seriously threatening injuries. Even that, as it turned out, was not career-threatening. I've had my share of pulls and strains, just as most players have, and that's when I've had to put some variations into my conditioning program.

When I've had a knee problem or back trouble so I couldn't run, I'd do the wind sprint part of the program in the deep end of a swimming pool. That consists of my running in place and not touching the bottom of the pool.

Conditioning for me is an all-year-round affair. I actually have two different programs: one is a maintenance program for in-season use, and the other is a strength program for the off-season. That consists of a lot of swimming and working with weights. Some players object to weights because they think they will get muscle-bound. I don't agree; I feel that if the work with the weights is done properly, it's a great strength builder.

Conditioning takes time and dedication. Some players don't seem to be able to find the time or have the dedication. I like to work out, and I set aside time for doing it and never let anything interfere. So I do believe one of the key factors in my longevity has been my day-after-day conditioning.

With all the attention and care I've given to my body, I'm really amazed at the way some young players have abused themselves. They've taken to not staying in shape, and some have gotten involved in drugs. I just have no idea why any athlete would behave in such a self-destructive way. To me, it makes absolutely no sense.

In January of 1987 I turned forty years old. That was a big number, but I considered myself to be fit, in better shape than I had been in a couple of seasons. I started thinking about playing in my twenty-first season in the major leagues, and I wondered about where all the years had gone.

A reporter called my home in Alvin. "How does it feel to be forty, Nolan," he asked, "and still be throwing that hardball?"

I gave him the standard kind of answer—that it felt really great, that I hoped I would be able to have a good season and help the Astros be competitive. The things I didn't say involved how much I loved baseball, the competition, the challenge. . . .

BING DEVINE:

I watched Stan Musial for a lot of years and was close to him when I was general manager of the St. Louis Cardinals. Stan realized that he was doing what he liked to an extreme and that he was lucky. He wasn't a million-dollar player like Nolan Ryan, but he was a $100,000 player, which was big money in those days.

Stan would say to me, "I can just picture the time when this locker will not be mine anymore. So as long as I can play and make it and not be embarrassed, I'm going to be here. I know once I get out of baseball, things are never going to be quite the same again."

Players like Stan Musial and Nolan Ryan realize things more than some of the others, and they keep meeting the challenge. Financially, they don't have that much to gain, but they're playing for pride and satisfaction, playing for immortality.

When the 1987 season began, I was pitching without pain, pitching with a good flow and rhythm. I was glad that during the off-season I had declined the suggestion by Dr. Jobe, the famous surgeon in Los Angeles, that I have surgery on my arm. Dr. Jobe had suggested that the only alternative might be the same kind of surgery for me that Tommy John had gone through. But I didn't think a ligament transplant in my arm was called for. I reasoned that something radical like that was a little premature for me. I decided the only way I'd go through with something like that was if all the other alternatives failed.

In a couple of games early in the 1987 season I threw over 135 pitches. I felt no pain. I had no problem. Then Hal Lanier came up to me with the news: "Dick Wagner has informed me that under no circumstances are you to throw more than 115 pitches in a game. When you reach 115, I've been told to take you out of the game."

That ticked me off. Once again a decision had been made without anyone's conferring with me. I requested a meeting. Dick Wagner, Hal Lanier, the team doctor, the trainer, and I met in an office in the Dome.

Wagner got into a whole preamble about how concerned he was about my arm. Then he pulled out a chart that indicated that in 1986 each time I started a game and threw more than 130 pitches, it appeared I had trouble pitching in my next start.

"The circumstances in 1986 were completely different," I told Dick. "In 1986," I explained to him, "I was pitching every fourth day and had an arm problem. The longer I pitched with that problem, the longer I pitched in '86, the more I aggravated it."

Dick listened to what I had to say. I knew what I said was only common sense, but none of what I said could convince Wagner. He had already made up his mind about the 115-pitch limit.

When you came right down to it, the whole thing was a labor-management situation. Wagner was management, and he was calling the shots on the team. I felt that the pitch-limit decision was unjust. It was a decision made by people who have never pitched, who were sitting there making observations based on charts and graphs. I wondered how they could have any inkling about what was going on with my elbow and my body. The people who knew the most about the situation—myself, Hal Lanier, and pitching coach Les Moss—should have been the ones to make the decision.

Throughout 1987 I pitched most of the time with that 115-pitch limit in a five-man rotation for the Astros. And all through the season the pitch limit was an ongoing problem, a continuing frustration for me.

More often than not, I'd be forced to leave the game after reaching my pitch limit. Then the other team would tie up the score or I wouldn't get a decision. Or we'd be trailing by a run or two, and I'd come out of the game. Our team would sometimes tie it up and I wouldn't get a decision. Or I'd leave trailing by a run or two and we wouldn't score and I'd get the loss.

One real frustrating game was against the Cardinals. I had a no-hitter for the first four innings. I had a shutout and gave up just three singles through six innings. I had thrown 115 pitches at that point. Hal took me out. I could easily have pitched longer. I was in a real groove and feeling no pain whatsoever.

Some people said the situation for me was like putting a thoroughbred horse in a race and then taking him out before he ever got the chance to get into the home stretch.

I realized what I was dealing with, so I wasn't going to argue and fight. Those were the rules Wagner had set down. I knew any ranting and raving by me would only cause distraction and dissension and take away from what we were trying to accomplish as a team—win ball games.

I was never one to shy away from a confrontation or a fight, but I've always realized there's no reason to get into things when it's counterproductive.

Hal Lanier was not to blame. I knew the position he was in. That pitch limit didn't come from Hal. As the manager of the Astros, he was just following Wagner's orders.

I never counted my pitches or thought about the limit or changed my style. If I threw 115 pitches the first four innings, then the game was over for me. That's the way it was, but it had to have an adverse effect. And it did.

Through most of the season I had one of the best earned run averages in baseball, had the best strikeout ratio per nine innings, and was always first or second in strikeouts. Yet I had a horrendous won and lost record.

Murray Chass did a column on me in the New York *Times* on August 13, when my record was 4–13. "Ryan's won-lost record is one of the most misleading pitching records in baseball history," he wrote. "At the age of 40, Ryan is pitching well enough to be a candidate for the Cy Young Award. . . ."

At that point I was eighth in the majors in ERA, second in hits allowed per nine innings, and leading the majors with 11.29 strikeouts per nine innings.

MILO HAMILTON:

I started in the big leagues as an announcer in 1953 with St. Louis and have been with Atlanta, Chicago, and Pittsburgh. I've been with Houston the last three years.

I've never seen anybody throw that hard that consistently in those numbers from the low nineties to high nineties and just keep on throwing the way Nolan Ryan does. . . .

A lot of times on a club you have an aging pitcher and he doesn't show good work habits or good personal habits. That's not the way it is with Nolan. He sets a fabulous example in both areas for the young players on the team. He just punishes himself to stay in shape.

We had a game against the Giants in August of 1987 where he was clocked at 98 miles per hour—and that's a forty-year-old man. There was a game in '87 where he struck out a pinch hitter, Harry Spilman, and the pitch he struck him out on was

96 miles an hour and that was the last pitch he threw in the game.

The most amazing thing to me about Ryan is that usually a guy that throws hard will have to start throwing some other things sometime after his thirty-fifth birthday, and the fastball sort of becomes incidental. Seaver was an example of that. Ryan has added some things, but he's still got that great fastball. And his curveball may be as good as it's ever been.

He's developed the circle change, but for him to call it a circle change is misleading. He grips it just like the other guys grip it, but he doesn't throw it to take something off. He throws it just like he was throwing a fastball, and with his great arm speed that thing is about 85 miles an hour. Some guys' fastballs aren't 85 miles an hour.

I saw him throw one in a game in August 1987 against Dave Martinez of the Chicago Cubs, a left-handed hitter. And I never saw a pitch move like that. Martinez just looked at it, that was all he could do. Some people say Nolan is scuffing the ball because it's such an unnatural pitch at that speed with all that action on it. The movement is what makes it such an effective pitch—it's a sinker now.

DALE MURPHY:

Nolan's the only pitcher you start thinking about two days before the game you face him. He's the bionic man—at age forty he's throwing the way he was when I first saw him.

Going into early September, we were chasing after the San Francisco Giants, who were in first place in our division. We had a chance to catch them—not a very good chance, but a chance.

I went out on September 9 to pitch against the Giants in the Dome and had one of my best games of the season. I struck out 16 in 8 innings, 10 of the last 12 batters, the last 5 in a row. It was the 11th time in 1987 that I struck out 10 or more batters in a game, the 173rd time I'd done it in my career.

In that game I recorded my 4,500th career strikeout. It was almost twenty-one years to the day, September 9, 1966, that I struck out my first major league batter—Pat Jarvis of the Atlanta Braves. That game gave me 226 strike-outs in just 176 innings of pitching that season, the major league lead. I got the win and we beat the Giants, 4–2.

Some of those Giant hitters were a little bit frustrated with all the heat I was throwing at them. Chili Davis was especially upset. I struck him out when he came up as a pinch hitter, and Chili broke his bat in half over his leg.

GLENN WILSON:

I know how Chili Davis felt. As a hitter, I have never faced anybody in my career—and I probably never will—that the night before you think so much about facing.

I always remember what Enos Cabell told me: "Just get as far back in the box as you can and start swinging when Ryan gets his leg up." That's about the way you do it.

I grew up in Houston down the road from where Nolan grew up. I remember us getting on the mound in high school and saying, "I'm Nolan Ryan." like kids used to say, "I'm Willie Mays."

Nolan faced my older brother when they were both in high school. I always joked around that he struck my brother out three times, and I owed him for that . . . but since then Nolan's struck me out more than three times.

I've hit two home runs off him, but I've told the guys on the Phillies, "If I'm lucky enough to hit another home run off him, do not come out and shake my hand. I'm gonna get around the bases so fast 'cause I don't want him to know who hit it."

When my career is over, and I sit down at the gas station or wherever, and people ask me, "What was one of your biggest moments?" I'll say, "Facing Nolan Ryan."

In the middle of September, Dick Wagner called me up. He informed me that after having discussions with the team doctor, he was going to expand my pitch limit to 125.

"That's fine," I said. I was surprised by the news, but there was no emotion on my part. I knew that Dick hadn't expected me to hold up physically all season as long as I had. That phone call settled the pitch limit controversy at least for 1987—and it was good to get it behind me.

With the new limit in place, I threw 123 pitches against the Giants, giving up just one run, in a nine-inning no-decision game in September. That game symbolized what happened all year long for me. It was the strangest season I've ever spent. When it began, I thought my biggest hurdle would be my elbow problem of 1986. As things turned out, that was my least concern.

I don't know if my stuff was as good as it was ten years ago, but I do know that I was a better pitcher. I kept the ball down better, worked the hitters better. I was more consistent in getting my curveball and my change-up over than I had been throughout my career.

The pitch limit, however, kept me from getting into the last few innings. Our middle relief was ineffective for most of the season, and I was in a spot in the rotation where we didn't score any runs. It was frustrating.

I wound up with an overall won-lost record of 8–16, yet my earned run average of 2.76 led the league. I also struck out 270 batters to lead the league and moved my all-time strikeout total to 4,547—more than a thousand more than the Walter Johnson record that I broke. I averaged 11.48 strikeouts per nine innings to set a new major league record in that category.

I won the National League Consort Control Pitcher Award with the highest rating in the majors based on hits given up, walks and strikeouts per nine innings, won and lost record, and ERA. Roger Clemens won the award in the American League, plus the Cy Young award. In 1986 Roger and Mike Scott won the Consort award and were also the Cy Young Award winners.

HAL LANIER:

I said all year that Nolan's record should've been turned around. With his final record at 8–16, that was not true anymore. I don't think anyone would've said that he should've been 16–8. Any knowledgeable baseball man, looking at his numbers, would say this pitcher should have 20 wins. If you looked at it that way, Nolan would have been the hands-down winner of the Cy Young Award.

There was some talk about my being considered as a Cy Young candidate. I knew, though, that a starting pitcher with a record below .500 was never honored. The won-lost record seems to be the deciding factor in the voters' minds. Since I didn't expect to get the award, I wasn't disappointed. But I don't think any pitcher in the league had been more effective than I was in 1987.

A bit after the season ended I had a meeting with Dick Wagner, who was being let go as Houston general manager. It was a cordial meeting, and Dick seemed to be relieved that he was finishing up. He was just fulfilling the duties that John McMullen had asked him to perform. My one-million-dollar contract with Houston was extended through the 1988 season. I felt good about that. I had come to Houston to finish my career there. I still am intent on finishing my career with the Astros.

I'll be forty-one years old going into the 1988 season, but I feel very optimistic, much more optimistic than I did about 1987 because I was going into that year with arm problems. I never set any goals for myself, but if our team gets some help and I stay healthy . . . well, you never know what can happen in the game of baseball.

EPILOGUE

In 1987 I received a lot of satisfaction when my mom was honored as the Little League "Mother of the Year" in Williamsport, Pennsylvania. She went up there with Ruth and Wendy. I had to pitch that day in Pittsburgh, so I couldn't attend.

My mother's receiving that award made me realize even more how much baseball has been an important part of the Ryan family life all these years. There's a poignancy to the whole situation that I find a little strange. I never thought that my kids would grow up and attend the same schools and play on the same baseball fields that I did in Alvin.

There have been only two real Little League fields in Alvin—the first one was built on the high school property. That field, built by the community, by my father and the other citizens of Alvin who volunteered their time, was used for about three or four years. I never played there, but my brother, Robert, did. Once the high school expanded, Schroeder Field—named after the family that donated the money for it—became the Little League field. That was the one I played on. My kids played on that same field.

I always anticipated that the day would come when I

would coach my kids in baseball. But because my career has lasted much longer than any of us thought it would, I haven't had the opportunity to coach them except in basketball during the off-season. Ruth coached Reid in Little League for one year and has coached Reese and Wendy in the younger leagues.

I haven't had as many opportunities as I would like to see my kids play because of my schedule, but I do get to see each one play about two to three times a year. We also play a lot of ball around the house. I pitch to them and throw batting practice. In 1986 we built a field out at the house, and in 1987 Reese's Little League team practiced there.

Our family of five is an echo of what I had growing up. Actually, I'm closer to my kids than my father was to me, my sisters, and my brother. He had to work so much that it took him away from his family. I have to be away a lot because of my baseball career, but thanks to my income level I'm able to take my family with me every opportunity I have. We do a lot of things together as a family. I take them on road trips a few times a year. Reese and Reid are bat boys. The kids have seen a lot of the United States and many different people, and it's been good for their educational development.

People expect my kids to have more baseball ability than the other kids, but they don't make comparisons to when I played as a kid. Alvin's changed a lot, and there aren't many people around from that time who saw me play. Both Reid and Reese have pitched and played the infield and outfield, pretty much what I did when I was a kid.

EPILOGUE

In the fall of '73, after I pitched the two no-hitters, the high school field that I had played on was renamed Nolan Ryan Field. Reid plays on that field now. In 1987, his first year at Alvin High, he pitched for the junior varsity. I saw him pitch twice, and he did very well for a freshman. I think they both have the potential to play on the high school and college level. After that, who knows? I would never have any of my children sign out of high school the way I did to play professional sports. I believe that youngsters should complete their college education first and then, if they have the ability, go on with a professional sports career.

To me the purpose of all sports is to teach the kids to play the game properly, to have fun, and hopefully get the opportunity to be on winning ball clubs. But if not, they're still learning the game. That's the way I view it. Unfortunately, it's not the way a lot of parents view it. They're trying to have their children fulfill some dream that they didn't realize.

At times—probably more times than I'm aware of—it's been hard on my kids being the children of Nolan Ryan, not only playing baseball, but in life in general. But I think it's been a good education for them. They've learned from the pressure and from the comparisons. It makes them more rounded in their development, and it'll help them deal with problems that they'll encounter in their lives.

My kids are part of one younger generation. Many of the players I compete against in baseball are part of another generation. And I'm one of the last ones left over from still another generation, the guys who came up to the majors in the 1960s. I guess those of us from my generation have more to look back to in baseball than we have to look ahead to. It's like the line in that tune "September Song" about the days dwindling down. . . .

How you're remembered in the history of baseball and how you want to be remembered are probably two different things. My numbers are going to influence people's opinions and thinking—they always have.

My won and lost record, my walks, my strikeouts—all those numbers are going to be factors in the way people will remember me. I don't worry about those things.

I want my teammates to remember me as a gamer, as a guy who just went out there and did his best each time out. I want them to remember me as a pitcher who did everything in his power to keep his team in a game, to give his team a chance to win. As a player, you respect what your peers think of you.

Somebody once labeled me as a .500 pitcher. I don't remember who did it, but he said, "Yeah, Nolan Ryan's got great stuff, but he's a .500 pitcher."

Some writers come up to me and ask, "How do you like the way 'they' describe you as a .500 pitcher?"

And I say "Who's 'they'? If you repeat that kind of stuff, then you're one of them." Those writers never appreciate my confronting them with that question.

Years ago that kind of label was more of an irritant to me than it is now. I realize now that people who say that kind of thing don't know much about baseball or haven't taken the time to investigate what has gone on in my career.

For me, some things never change. I'm still throwing 70 percent fastballs, sometimes 80 percent, the same ratio I've always thrown. I'm mixing in a few sinkers now. I started fooling around with the sinker in 1986 when my elbow was hurting. I just turn the ball over. It looks like the fastball, but it'll drop if I keep it down.

It's a challenge for me to continue to perform and still be the same style of pitcher I've always been: a power pitcher, throwing heat.

I have no regrets about my career. I'm the all-time leader in strikeouts, no-hitters, strikeouts per nine innings. I'm the only pitcher in history to have struck out more than 2,000 batters in each league. I'm also one of only three pitchers to have led both leagues in strikeouts in a season.

I'm disappointed that I don't have a better won and lost record, but I've won twenty-five more games than Whitey Ford did, and just seven fewer than Jim Palmer. I'm one of eight pitchers to have won 20 games for a last-place team.

Lots of things in the game have been out of my control. In my twenty-one years in the big leagues, I've played on only five division or league championship teams. Twice I pitched for last-place teams, and five times I was on next-to-last-place teams. Three times clubs I pitched for finished last in team batting. Most of the other clubs I've played for were not exactly loaded with hefty hitters, either. Until the last few years with the Astros, I've never been on a team with a strong bullpen. My attitude is that I always gave it my best even though there were times when things just didn't work out the way I wanted them to.

It's been one long gallop for me from Alvin High School through two decades plus in the majors. Looking back over it all, lots of things kind of run together: the dedication of Jim Watson and Red Murff, who did so much to get me started; the kindliness of my first pro manager, Pete Pavelick; the help and encouragement of Jeff Torborg, Tom Morgan, Harry Dalton, and Gene Autry, who gave a young kid a chance to show what he had; the humor of Norm Cash; the friendship of Jimmy Reese; the professionalism of Tom Seaver; the steadiness of Phil Garner, Alan Ashby, Bill Doran; the support of the fans at Shea Stadium and Anaheim and the Dome, and especially the support the fans have given me over the years.

All kinds of images and experiences remain within me: the rebirth of spring training; the workouts; the reaching back for a little more thunder on the throw and the smack of the ball into the leather of the catcher's glove; the hush and roar of so many crowds; the long summers moving across America; the intense one-on-one encounters with the tough hitters; the frenzy of pennant races; the sadness of seasons winding down; the gallery of players, managers, coaches, media people, umpires that make up the world within a world that is baseball; and the satisfaction of games well played, records set, and milestones achieved.